JAMES MCCARTHY is the former Deputy Director (Scotland) of the Nature Conservancy Council and is a Board Member of its successor, Scottish Natural Heritage, representing that organisation as a director of the Edinburgh Green Belt Trust. One time Vice-Chairman of the Secretary of State's Working Group on Environmental Education, he is currently Chairman of the Environmental Youth Work Development Project Scotland, and a member of the Scottish Council for National Parks and of the Scottish Environmental Education Council. He is a member of the Forestry Commision's Mid Scotland Regional Advisory Committee.

Previously a forest officer in East Africa and widely travelled in Europe, Canada, USA and Australia, James McCarthy's 30 years in active land and conservation management at home and overseas enables him to take a wide perspective on his native country as environmental consultant, writer, lecturer and guide. He is the author of *Wild Scotland* (Scottish Tourist Board 1995; Revised, expanded and updated edition Luath Press 1998) and of articles on the wildlife of Scotland for Scottish Tourist Board's *Scotland: Where to Go and What to See*, among several other publications. He is committed to promoting Scotland as a unique environment which he believes is often under-rated, and to encourage sustainable tourism through holistic education, connecting natural heritage, history and culture for a deeper understanding of the country.

Scotland is the country above all others that I have seen, in which a man of imagination may carve out his own pleasures, there are so many inhabited solitudes.

Dorothy Wordsworth: Journal, August 1803

An Inhabited Solitude:
Scotland, Land and People

JAMES McCARTHY

Luath Press Limited

EDINBURGH

www.luath.co.uk

First Published as *Scotland: the Land and its Uses*
by Chambers, Edinburgh 1994
Revised, Expanded and Updated 1998

This book is made from
low chlorine pulps produced in a
low energy, low emission manner
from renewable forests and from
recycled materials, the latter comprising
at least 50% of the pulps used.

Printed and bound by
Gwasg Dinefwr Press Ltd., Llandybie

Typeset in 10.5 point Sabon by
S. Fairgrieve, Edinburgh, 0131 658 1763

Contents

NATURAL
FACTORS

Shetland

HUMAN
ACTIVITIES

Orkney

GEOLOGY
CLIMATE
LANDSCAPE
VEGETATION

TOWNSCAPES
&
ARCHITECTURE

Lewis

Harris

Inverness

Aberdeen

Skye

SCOTTISH
ENVIRONMENT

Mull

Dundee

Islay

Glasgow

Edinburgh

INDUSTRY

SETTLEMENT
&
BUILDINGS

Arran

Dumfries

TRANSPORT
&
SERVICES

SCENERY
&
WILDLIFE

RURAL LAND USE

Scotland and the influences on its environment

Introduction

Scotland is a paradox. A tiny country on the north west fringe of Europe, it yet has a singular identity which is recognised throughout the world. The most potent symbols of that identity - scenery, history and culture - have their origins in the least inhabited part of the country. It has consistently been at the forefront of advances in science and technology, yet clings proudly to its unique traditions. Espousing the rights of the common man from early in its history, it tolerates archaic feudal laws and customs which have been banished elsewhere. Dedicated to democracy, it has only recently taken the first tentative steps towards restoring its ancient parliament. Inordinately proud of its heritage, it almost allowed its Celtic culture to die. Rich in natural beauty, it has so far eschewed any recognised international designation for its finest landscapes. Many of these and other paradoxes are demonstrated by the history of the land and man's relationship to it, as exemplified by the title of this book and Dorothy Wordsworth's observation at the beginning of the 19th century. One of the purposes of this book is to explain how this has come about as part of the story of our increasing control over the environment from earliest times to the present, and to explore some of the issues relating to this. It attempts to give a coherent and mainly factual account of the main elements of Scotland's unique environment, answering a number of questions posed by visitors, but rarely if ever addressed by the standard guidebooks. The visitor to Scotland will find no lack of the lattter, or works on the history and culture of the country, and there is specialized writing on everything from whisky to bagpipes. What is not so easy to find is concise, factual information on the basic geography of the land and its use.This book fills that gap, by providing a general picture of the environment of Scotland, its most distinctive characteristics, and the way in which its physical resources have been used against that background. That environment cannot be restricted to the natural one, but must include the man-made towns and cities where most people live and work. Above all, it demonstrates what an astonishingly diverse country this is and how it could, with its natural and human resources, provide a model of the balance between sustainable development and conservation.

It is intended firstly as an introduction to the country's geology, climate, landscapes, wildlife, and human history, and secondly to explain how its agriculture, forestry, manufacturing industry and energy resources have been developed. It describes, for example, the link between the glaciation of the country and the development of hydropower, the expansion of new forests within the limits of a northern climate, and how soils and temperature have restricted lowland cereal farming. It links the geology and location of mineral resources to the historic concentration of industry within the central Lowlands, and shows how this axis has changed with the discovery of North Sea oil. Particular sections are dedicated to the different historical elements in its population make-up, and their settlements.The increasingly important tourist industry and the measures necessary to conserve its renowned landscapes and wildlife are discussed. The final chapter focuses on some of the major issues concerning the future of the land, including ownership and the management of the countryside, and the place of environmental education. Locations and sites relating to the topics covered with public information facilities for visitors are listed .

Near the completion of the draft of this book, the results of the 1997 referendum confirmed that by the time of the new millennium, Scotland would have its own Parliament. The result itself indicated that there was a new mood of confidence abroad in the country.While foreign journalists seemed astonished by the soberness with which the announcement was greeted, there seemed little doubt about the sense of quiet satisfaction that at long last the country is to be at least partially in control of its own destiny. At a time when there are increasing pressures towards homogeneity and conformity to the demands of the multinational marketplace, there is hope that those distinctive elements of Scottish life and culture, including the independence of its distinctive institutions, will be maintained. Certainly, the new Parliament will be responsible for the environment of Scotland with the opportunity of land reform and new approaches to the protection and management of an incomparable countryside to meet the needs of the 21st century.

James McCarthy
March 1998

CHAPTER I

The Land - Some Facts and Figures

The land of Scotland hath plenty of vytail and corn but not abundant as in the realm of England, for this land is in many places steryll.

Roger Barlow – *A Brief Summe of Geographie* (1540)

SCOTLAND LIES BETWEEN LATITUDES 54 and 61 north, and an imaginary line drawn east from Shetland would strike Bergen in Norway. In the opposite direction, the line would pass through the southern tip of Greenland before cutting through the middle of Hudson's Bay to touch southern Alaska. It is undoubtedly a northern country but, bounded by the Atlantic Ocean on the west and the North Sea on the east, it is mild enough to maintain ice-free coasts during the winter months. Because of its northern position it enjoys long summer twilights, and at midsummer there is no complete darkness. It lies entirely between 0 and 10 degrees longitude, the 5 degree line running virtually through the middle of the country. The border with England partly follows the River Tweed from the North Sea coast, then crosses the summits of the Cheviot Hills, before the Solway Firth clearly separates the two countries in the west.

On a world scale, Scotland is a tiny country; at its narrowest, between the Forth and the Clyde, it is only 41km/25miles from east to west, and very few places are more than 64km/40miles from the sea. With a total land area of 787,830sq km/30,405sq miles, Scotland is approximately 34 per cent of the total area of Britain and about three-fifths the size of England. Although the mainland distance from north to south at its maximum is a mere 440km/275miles, the inclusion of the northern isles of Orkney and Shetland extends this by almost half as much again – Shetland is in fact closer to the Arctic Circle than to London and its nearest railway station is Bergen in Norway!

Largely because of the highly indented west coast and its islands, Scotland has a disproportionately long coastline of 10,000km/6,214miles, but the developed length is under

500km/457miles. There are almost 800 islands (of which only 130 are inhabited), ranging from substantial land areas such as the Northern Isles (Orkney and Shetland) and Western Isles, which total 4,126sq km/1,593sq miles, to small groups of off-shore rocks. There are five major estuaries, or firths – the Forth, Tay, Moray, Clyde and Solway – and the west coast is characterised by numerous long sea lochs, often penetrating more than 50km/31 miles into the mountain hinterland. Scotland is mainly mountainous, with 65 per cent of the country above 120m/400ft. It contains the highest mountain in Britain, Ben Nevis (1,344m/4,408ft), and 284 mountains classified as 'Munros' (i.e. above 914m/3000ft) – the Cairngorm Mountains form the greatest area in Britain above this altitude. Hill ground supports rough grazing, the largest (70 per cent) single agricultural land use, which covers over 40,000sq km/15,500sq miles – more than half the total land area of Scotland. More than any other feature, these mountains characterise the image of Scotland's countryside, its bens and glens.

Next to the mountains, the lochs and rivers are the features most closely associated with the popular picture of Scotland's landscape. There are reckoned to be over 30,000 lochs, inland bodies of water covering 2.3 per cent of the country; (in Britain as a whole, freshwater covers 1 per cent of the land area) in the Highlands of Scotland this rises to 5 per cent. There are 6,628 mainland rivers in Scotland, with a total length of 47,984km/29,801 miles. The major river systems are the Tay, Spey, Clyde, Tweed, Dee, Don and Forth. Almost 98 per cent of the total length of these rivers is classified as unpolluted, and they provide 12 per cent of Scotland's water supply, almost all of the remainder coming from 355 lochs and reservoirs, with only 3 per cent coming from underground sources. Only 1 per cent of the available surface water in Scotland is used for water supply, leaving a huge excess over demand.

With a population of only 5 million (about one-eleventh of the total British population), Scotland is one of the most sparsely populated countries in continental Europe. The average density is 65 persons per square kilometre, but this falls to 8 persons in Highland Council area, the largest area covered by a local authority in the UK. By contrast, the Lothians, including the capital Edinburgh, have a density of 427 persons per square kilometre. The population is more unevenly distributed than that of any other country in Europe, with the four main cities of Glasgow,

Edinburgh, Aberdeen and Dundee together having over 1.5 million people, one third of the total population. Some 80 per cent of that total live in the Central Belt stretching from the Firth of Clyde to the Firth of Forth. However, 45 per cent of the population live in settlements of fewer than 25,000 people. Urban areas are only 3 per cent of the total land mass, and the remainder is classified as countryside, approximately 17 per cent of which is in the environmentally sensitive category.

A marked feature of Scotland is the history inherent in its landscape, from Pictish stones to medieval castles, often in settings which have changed remarkably little over the ages. As late as 1750 almost half the population lived north of the Tay, but a combination of emigration overseas and the drift towards the new industrial centres denuded many of the Highland areas of their communities over the next century. The union of Scotland with England, first under one Crown in 1603 and subsequently, in 1707, by the joining of Parliaments, not only ended centuries of warfare between the Scots and the English, but also gave Scotland access to the developing Empire. Emigration has been a feature of Scottish history over the last 250 years and, combined with the decline in birthrate, continues to have its effect on the population. The shifts in population and the major changes in the industrial base of the country over this period are reflected in the settlement pattern and the significant changes in the economy and land use.

CHAPTER 2

A Rocky Country

They had been crumpled up like a pile of carpets.

Sir Archibald Geikie – *geologist* (1835-1924)

GIVEN ITS SIZE, SCOTLAND'S geology is astonishingly varied, and the country has produced geologists who have made discoveries of world-wide significance. Visitors come to Scotland simply to examine the classic sites identified by James Hutton, Hugh Miller, Charles Lapworth and Archibald Geikie (quoted above on the landscape of the Southern Uplands). The story of the laying down of the foundations of Scotland encompasses vast volcanic eruptions, submersion under the sea, great earth movements and tidal waves, and enormous sheets of ice covering the whole land. It is a process of construction, demolition and renewal on a gigantic scale. The history of Scotland's rocks, some of them among the oldest on earth, goes back almost 3,000 million years.

Some 500 million years ago, Scotland was on the edge of a vast ancient northern continent which linked Scandinavia, Greenland and North America. Huge sheets of eroded sands from this continent emerged to form the base rocks of grey and pink gneiss over much of northern Scotland. To hold in the hand a pebble of banded gneiss from the Atlantic shore of the western Hebrides and realise that it might have come from the coast of Nova Scotia more than 500 million years ago is a mind-boggling experience. We know from the fossil record that, at one time, more than 450 million years ago, Scotland lay south of the equator and was separated from England by an ancient sea 1,500km/900 miles wide. There were periods when it was a desert, others when it was covered by tropical rainforest and, at times, under an ice cap.

The last glaciation, about 10,000 years ago, is the most recent significant event: if Scotland's total geological time span is considered as a 24 hour period, it took place less than a second ago, or in the "blink of a geological eyelash" as one author has it. There have been many previous ice epochs – at least five in the last three million years, and this ice, over a kilometre thick, has greatly altered almost every aspect of Scotland's landscape. The vast amounts of rock and ice deposited by the melting glaciers radically changed the courses of rivers, while enormous lochs, such as Loch Lomond, were created by the gouging action of the glaciers. Mountain tops were scraped off, corries and high-altitude ice lochs were formed and valleys were deepened and widened. The distinctive second beach levels above the present beaches round much of Scotland's coast are the result of the submersion of the land under its weight of ice; when the ice melted the land rose again, and continues to do so.

A feature of present day Scotland is the extensive peat deposits covering much of the north and west, the result of a cool, moist climate and widespread acid rocks which inhibit vegetation decomposition and soil formation. The peatlands of Caithness and Sutherland alone represent seven per cent of the total world resource. Although there are soils as fertile as any other in Britain, particularly those derived from the rich red sandstones along the east coast, these are localised. Elsewhere, the geology of the country often produces shallow sandy or organic soils with poor drainage, both of which are often low in plant food, interspersed with pockets of much richer soils developed from localised limestone deposits. High rainfall in the west rapidly washes out such nutrients and iron may be deposited as a hard impervious layer under peat, preventing tree root penetration.

A look at even the simplest geological map of the country shows by its range of colours the sheer diversity of different strata, from the greatly altered Pre-Cambrian rocks in the north west, to the more recent volcanic lavas and the economically important marine sediments from the Carboniferous period of the central

Lowlands. Despite this complexity, there are four quite distinct geological regions, separated by the major fault and thrust lines which cross the country, mainly from north-east to south-west. The most obvious is the Highland Boundary Fault, which separates highland from lowland Scotland, running from Stonehaven on the Kincardine coast to the island of Arran in the south-west passing en route through the middle of Loch Lomond, where it shows up as a line of wooded islands. The highland area is divided by another thrust line 161km/100miles long from Loch Eriboll in Sutherland to the Sleat Peninsula on Skye, separating the extreme northwest (including the Outer Hebrides) from the northern and central Highlands dominated by the Cairngorm massif. The southern side of the central Lowlands is marked by the Southern Uplands Fault, which is less obvious, although the appearance of these Border Hills to the south, on quite different geological strata, is distinctive. The Great Glen, in which Loch Ness sits, runs southwest from Inverness and near Fort William is penetrated by Loch Lhinne.

North-West Highlands and Islands

Of these four regions, the geology of the far north-west has produced the most dramatic and distinctive scenery. Here are the oldest of the country's rocks, the Lewisian gneiss, representing an ancient landscape thrust upwards from the lower earth's crust for a distance of 19km/12miles, twice the height of Mount Everest. The gneiss was overlain by massive beds of red pebbly sandstones, of the type visible today in the Torridon district. These sandstones, up to five miles thick, were laid down by huge river systems of the great north-west continent of which Scotland was then a part. The enormous forces of glacial erosion have cut through the strata to isolate the fantastic shapes of the peaks of Suilven and Canisp, rising like towering castles from a rocky plain. In the Outer Hebrides the Lewisian gneiss created a barren, low-lying terrain of exposed grey rock, interspersed with literally thousands of pools and deep peat deposits. This pattern of treeless rock and water, so obviously worn down by the ice and penetrated by the sea, is unlike any other land formation in Europe outside western Norway, with which it was once connected.

Another type of mountain scenery occurs on Skye, where the

6

quite different igneous gabbro rock has been worn away to create the ridges and pinnacles of the Cuillins, a Mecca for skilled climbers. To the north of the same island, spectacular lava flows have formed dramatic coastal cliffs, and subsequent massive land-slides are demonstrated inland by the strange, distorted shapes of Quiraing and the Storr, where the sediments below have broken up and erosion has left isolated towers of rock. Much of the North West Highlands were covered by lava 60 million years ago, some of the beds, such as those on Mull, about 1,800m/5400ft thick, at a time when North America was separating from Scotland with the widening of the Atlantic. We know from fossil evidence that Scotland enjoyed a much warmer climate at this time, with tropi-cal plants and animals flourishing. Even hotter was the period around 260 million years ago, when the New Red Sandstone was formed under desert conditions, and the Minch, separating the Outer Hebrides from mainland Scotland, was created by gigantic faulting.

Northern and Central Highlands

The whole of this large, mainly mountainous area north of the Highland Boundary Fault is dominated by metamorphic rocks which have been greatly altered by heat and pressure. These are the Dalradian and Moine series of schists and quartzites laid down between 600 and 1,200 million years ago, the base material into which other igneous rocks have been pushed. They have been sub-ject to enormous folding during the Caledonian mountain-build-ing era, when the ranges may have been on a Himalayan scale before being massively eroded and subsequently shaped by the ice into the landscape we know today.

During Devonian times, some 350 to 400 million years ago, the great granite massifs such as the Cairngorms were pushed under the Dalradian/Moine series and surfaced after erosion of the covering material. It is in this granite that the rare and beautiful crystals of beryl and Cairngorm stone are found. The scale of the high Cairngorm plateau makes it the most extensive area of arctic climate in Britain, with some of the finest examples of glaciation features, such as the great U-shaped valley of the Lairig Ghru, linking Speyside and Deeside.

In the extreme north-east of this area, including the coast of

Caithness and Orkney, lie the sedimentary rocks of the Old Red Sandstone and the Jurassic. The sandstone flags are a distinctive feature of the countryside, where they are used as field boundaries, and also form spectacular coastal cliffs which erode readily into dramatic geos (chasms), caves, blowholes and off-shore sea stacks such as the Old Man of Hoy. Erosion of the joints in the coastal rocks provides very suitable cliff nesting sites for the huge numbers of colonial sea birds around the Orkney coast.

The Central Lowlands

The broad band of the Midland valley stretching across the waist of Scotland is notable for its commercially valuable Carboniferous sediments which have fuelled much of Scottish industry, especially coal and limestone.The whole area was on the southern limit of a vast supercontinent now partially covered by the Atlantic. The Old Red Sandstone again appears to the north of this belt in the rich red fields of Angus and Kincardine (where it achieved a depth of up to 6,000m/19,683ft) and around the Forth in East Lothian. Much of the original material in this valley came from the higher ground on either side, before being covered, often by volcanic material, at many different times; there are no less than 1,000 volcanic vents in the Central Belt alone, and in northeast Fife there is a greater concentration of volcanic vents than anywhere else in Europe. Their remains, set in the surrounding mass of Old Red Sandstone and Carboniferous rocks and eroded by ice action, show up clearly in this undulating agricultural landscape. The shallow seas of Carboniferous times laid down the wide variety of economic deposits on which the wealth of the region was founded, not only coal and limestone, but also ironstone, sandstone, clay and oil-bearing shales from the Lower Carboniferous, all of which have been exploited.

During the period of the formation of these strata, much of central Scotland was tropical swamp, not dissimilar to those of present-day Florida. These rain forests and swamps were inundated from time to time by warm seas, supporting coral reefs, which eventually provided limestone, and sea muds. Both of these later yielded the fossils of extinct plants and animals, including the world's earliest known reptile. Fossilised remains of tropical trees from this period can be seen in Glasgow's Victoria Park. Many of the buildings of that city are made of the New Red Sandstone from the later desert period. Unlike England, the whole of Scotland was subject to massive glaciation and even the lowland landscape shows definite ice features. Among these are the low hummocks and ridges of sand and gravel left behind by the melting ice sheets. These deposits, of considerable economic importance for quarrying and construction, can be seen throughout the lowlands, but especially around Carstairs and Biggar.

Most of the geological features of this part of Scotland can be seen in and around the capital city of Edinburgh, which has a unique association with the development of the science of geology and is a Mecca for geologists from around the world. It was here that the father of modern geology, James Hutton, demonstrated his theories of cyclical destruction and renewal of the earth's crust over periods of time never before contemplated. A Berwickshire farmer, he was also a leading figure of the Scottish Enlightenment in the latter half of the 18th century, and based his great work Theory of the Earth on his investigation of the mighty volcanoes that erupted from the tropical seas around Edinburgh over 400 million years ago. All the hills in this area are of volcanic origin, but Arthur's Seat is especially spectacular with its sequences of lava and ash intruded by dolerite sills, clearly visible in Salisbury Crags. Molten rocks forming in volcanic vents have produced the well-known 'Samson's Ribs', the basaltic formation similar to that of Fingal's Cave off Mull. The neighbouring rock on which the castle sits. together with the Royal Mile linking it to Holyrood Palace, is a classic 'crag and tail formation', isolated by the eastward-flowing ice sheet which swept away the softer surrounding sediments.

To further establish Edinburgh's claim to geological fame, in 1840 the Swiss geologist Louis Agassiz for the first time correctly identified ice scratches on a rock now known as the Agassiz Rock, on Blackford Hill within the city boundary. This revolutionised ideas on the impact and extent of ice action over the whole of the Scottish landscape, confirmed when Agassiz saw the shores of vanished glacial lakes at the 'Parallel Roads' of Glen Roy. The same ice gouged out the hollows of the lakes and marshes which previously occupied Princes Street Gardens and the Meadows. At the end of the Ice Age, the sea was 40m/120ft higher, lapping around the base of Calton Hill at the east end of Princes Street, and the melting of the ice created a raised beach of 10m/30ft, which can be seen around the city's Forth shore. Falls in sea levels altered the river profiles, as the River Almond and the Water of Leith cut new gorges through the sediments. During the Carboniferous period, some of the sediments in marine and lake basins formed the Midlothian coalfield to the east of the city, while to the west, different deposits produced the oil shale that was to become a significant industry in the latter half of the 19th century.

The Southern Uplands

These softly rounded green hills between the Central Belt and the English border are relatively uniform in their predominant sedimentary shales and slates from the Silurian/Ordovician period between 400 and 500 million years ago, but were worn down from an older landscape probably of pre-Jurassic age. The rocks have also been very much altered by volcanic activity, especially towards the end of the Upper Old Red Sandstone period, creating such distinctive isolated hills as the Eildons in the middle Tweed Valley. The rounded appearance has been formed by ice action on these Lower Paleozoic rocks, and at the Devil's Beef Tub above Moffat there is a classic example of valley deepening by glaciation. The shales and slates were formed from marine sediments and muds under the ancient ocean which separated Scotland from England. It was the closing of this ocean, under enormous lateral

pressure, that produced the massive folding of the Silurian strata, which can be seen so spectacularly on the high sea cliffs north of St. Abbs – one can only stand and wonder at this classic demonstration of the power of earth movements, so aptly described by Archibald Geikie in the quotation above.

On the border itself the Cheviot range rises sharply,

great masses of volcanic rock from the Old Red Sandstone age. There are also outcrops of Carboniferous rocks, and isolated occurrences of coal seams on the southern edge of the Pentlands and at Sanquar, north-west of Dumfries. Along the Galloway coast the lowlands are of varied origin, but around Stranraer and Dumfries is New Red Sandstone, which is actively quarried at Locharbriggs near Dumfries. Upstanding granite masses create a "highlands-in-miniature" landscape in the Glen Trool district and occur elsewhere at the Cairnsmore of Fleet and at Criffel near Dumfries. The whole of the Borders area is noted for important fossil beds, tracing the develoment of spore-bearing plants, to seed plants, fish and insects, from which the Borders geologist Charles Lapworth made discoveries of world-wide significance on the dating of the rock sequence in the latter half of the 19th century.

CHAPTER 3

The Changing Sky

So this is your Scotland. It is rather nice, but dampish and Northern and one shrinks a trifle inside one's skin. For these countries, one should be an amphibian.

D H Lawrence – *letter to the Hon Dorothy Brett*, 14 August 1928

IT IS SAID THAT whereas other countries have a climate, Scotland has weather. Changeability is the predominant feature, with weather fronts constantly pushing in from the Atlantic to the west. The climate is cool and moist, without extremes of heat or cold, but with many windy days. The sky is often as dramatic as the land, with constantly changing cloudscapes and patterns of light and shade. Especially between showers, the contrast between rain clouds and clear sky can result in an unusual clarity of light and remarkable visibility.

There is good evidence to suggest that since the last Ice Age there have been considerable fluctuations in the climate, and that in Stone Age times a warmer period allowed communities to develop at relatively high altitudes. Subsequent cooler, wetter weather probably caused population movements and certainly created the conditions for the widespread development of peat, particularly in the west. Visitors to Scotland remark on the scarcity of trees on our mountains, and although there are other factors, the maximum natural tree line of about 500m/1,500ft is primarily the result of exposure, often demonstrated by isolated trees, stunted and wind-bent in unsheltered situations. By contrast, in sheltered situations on the west coast, the warmth of the Gulf Stream allows palms to flourish in luxuriant sub-tropical gardens.

Rainfall

A popular misconception is that all parts of Scotland receive very high rainfall. In fact much of the east coast has an annual average of under 800mm/31in, and during the main summer months of May, June, July and August, a total of less than 250mm/10in which compares well with the drier districts of the south of England. The average annual rainfalls for Edinburgh and London are almost the same, just as the figures for the wetter parts of the Highlands are similar to those of the Lake District. There are low-lying coastal areas of Scotland, including Nairn, Arbroath and Dunbar, which actually record an annual rainfall of less than 600mm/23.6in. On the other hand, the east coast can frequently be swathed in the summer sea mists, or haar, while inland areas are enjoying warm sunshine.

The fact that so much of Scotland is mountainous means however that a relatively large proportion of the country does receive heavy rainfall of over 1,600mm/63in annually with frequent low cloud levels and hill fog. (One of my most memorable holidays was of camping on Skye when it rained non-stop for the entire week!) A feature of Scottish weather, in the absence of rain, is an overcast sky which gives a typically grey colour to the landscape, even in high summer. There is marked variation between the seasons, particularly on the west coast. The total rainfall between February and June is often just over half that in the period between September and January: a good reason for visiting the west of Scotland in spring and early summer. Summer thunderstorms are relatively rare. Due to plentiful rain and ample supply of surface water, Scotland has not suffered from the droughts affecting many other parts of Britain in recent years, and is fortunate in not relying upon underground water supplies.

Temperature and sunshine

Since few areas in Scotland are more than 64km/40miles from the coast, the whole country is insulated by the surrounding sea. Although Scotland is on a similar latitude to southern Alaska, its estuaries do not freeze in winter. The temperature tends to decrease from west to east, although this can be considerably modified by altitude (about 0.6°C for every 100m/328ft in height). This east/west difference is actually more significant than variation in latitude.

Temperature ranges are greatest inland; on the coast there are relatively small changes in daily temperature. The lowest temperature record is held by the inland village of Braemar at -27.2°C. Surprisingly, on the coldest nights the lowest temperatures are often to be found in the inland valley bottoms, and not on the mountain tops. The mean daily minimum temperature in January ranges across Scotland from -0.5°C to 2.5°C and the maximum from 5.5°C to 7.5°C, which is very similar to many parts of England. In summer, however, temperatures are usually a few degrees lower than those south of the border, ranging from a mean daily maximum in July of 14.5°C to 17.5°C and a minimum of 9.5°C to 11.5°C, the latter being recorded most frequently on the Berwickshire coast. The coolest summer weather is found in Lewis in the Outer Hebrides. Visitors from continental Europe and North America claim to feel colder in our relatively 'mild' climate, despite the absence of very low air temperatures, because of the penetrating damp, often compounded by wind.

It is also true that the west coast has some of the highest sunshine records in late spring and early summer, with May often being the sunniest month. The island of Tiree is notable for having an average daily record of 6.9 hours of bright sunshine in this month and also holds the record of 329 hours for a single month, although the best average annual total is claimed by Dunbar on the East Lothian coast. Day length is a more significant factor for crop growers: although the growing season is short, and winter days are only a few hours long, the northern summer days can make up for this. In Lerwick in Shetland for example, at a latitude of over 60°N, sunrise is at 03.38 and sunset at 22.34 (British Summer Time) on 21 June, giving a day four hours longer than its equivalent in London. On the longest day, there is really no complete darkness in the north of Scotland: it is possible to play golf at midnight in northern Shetland.

Wind

It is said that you can recognise an Edinburgh man anywhere in the world - before he turns a street corner, he automatically clutches his hat ...

The highest gust of wind recorded in Scotland was 150 knots (over 278kmph/173mph at 1,245m/4,085ft in the Cairngorms on 20 March 1986 – wind speeds increase very significantly with altitude. Wind is a feature of Scottish weather in general, as a result of the major Atlantic depressions which pass over Scotland, although lengthy periods of strong winds are not usual on the west coast during the summer months. It is the west and northern coasts, including Orkney and Shetland, which have the highest frequency of gales during the winter, with westerlies predominant. Lerwick, for example, has an annual average of over 47 gale-ridden days. The force and persistence of the wind above 500m/1,500ft is shown by the indigenous vegetation, which rarely exceeds a few inches in height on the higher hills.

Snow

In coastal regions of Scotland snow rarely lies for more than 10 days in the year, while in some of the north-facing high-level corries it can persist in small patches throughout the year - in one corrie in the Cairngorms the snow has melted completely only twice this century. Snowfall increases markedly with height, and over the Drummochter Pass at 460m/1,380ft on the main A9 road between Perth and Inverness, snow lies for an average 70 days in any one year. Although snowfall is often greater in the west of the country, it tends to lie longer in the east. In Scotland, in contrast to Continental Europe, the frequency of winds results in accumulations of snow on leeward slopes and wherever obstructions (such as fences) occur. As a consequence, drifting and blockage of roads is not infrequent, especially on the notorious Cockbridge to Tomintoul Road in Aberdeenshire. Even in mountain areas however, other than on the highest summits, snow cover is very variable, and a mild wind can remove it in a matter of hours, to the chagrin of skiers. To demonstrate the fickleness of Scottish weather I frequently show a slide of a foot of snow on either side of a road a few miles outside Edinburgh with vehicle headlights shafting through a leaden sky – taken at 2.0 p.m. on 15th May!

The effects of global warming on the climate of Scotland are quite uncertain, but ironically, we could be subject to cooler weather if the predictions of melting glaciers in the Arctic prove true, with the possibility of an increase in southern icebergs with colder waters pushing the Gulf Stream further south. The effects of this might conceivably produce a mini-Ice Age, with Scotland experiencing similar weather to other areas in the world on a comparable latitude (such as Labrador) albeit modified by our island situation. Other predictions include an increase in rainfall and turbulence. As the coast of Scotland relative to the southern parts of Britain is rising, especially towards the north-west, we may be less affected by rises in sea level and consequent sea flooding.

CHAPTER 4

Natural Scotland

Of Scotland I persave the properties
Of this countrie the great commodities.
First the aboundance of fishes in our seas,
And fructual mountanis for our bestiale;
And, for our cornis, mony lusty vale;

The rich Riveris, pleasand and profitabill;
The lustie lochis, with fish of sindry kindis;
Huntin, hawking, for nobillis convenabill;
Forrestis full of Dae, Rae, Hartis and Hyndis
The fresh fountainis, whose holesum cristal strandis
Refreshis so the fair flursite green meadis;
So laik we no thing that to nature needis.

Sir David Lindsay (1490-1555) – *The Dreme: Of the Realm of*
Scotland

SCOTLAND CAN RIGHTLY CLAIM to be one of the most unspoilt
countries in Europe, with great sweeps of open mountain and
moorland, large deep lochs, and some of the cleanest rivers in the
world. Its coastal and island scenery is famous, and the general
impression of visitors is of a country with ample wild space and
great natural beauty. Scotland has a rich and varied wildlife
because of its great diversity of natural habitats, although almost
all of these have been modified to some extent by man with the
exception of the steepest sea cliffs and mountain crags. Several of
these habitats are of international importance, either because they
are scarce on a global scale or because they are inhabited by a high
proportion of the world's population of particular species. The
animals that were found Scotland in the period immediately after
the last Ice Age included the elk, brown bear, bison, wild boar,
wolf and beaver, and many others which have since disappeared -
the result partly of changes in climate, but equally of the destruction of natural habitats by man, especially the sheltering forest
which at one time clothed much of the country.

Scotland, in common with the rest of Britain, has a much reduced flora and fauna compared with Europe; when the North Sea, created by the melting of glaciers, broke the land bridge between Britain and its Continental neighbours, many species lost the opportunity to colonise areas that were becoming habitable with the improvement in climate. Generally, because of its latitude and island situation, Scotland's plants and animals have many similarities to others in the north-east Atlantic region, such as Scandinavia, modified by the warming effect of the Gulf Stream, which allows sub-tropical plants to survive on the west coast.

Perhaps the first impression for a visitor to Scotland will be the sheer amount of countryside, and the relative lack of people, compared with further south. Away from the more industrialised central belt, the environment is still predominantly rural, with hill country never far away, either as gently rolling moorland or as spectacular mountain scenery which can be awesome in scale. Spring and autumn colours are especially vivid, from the striking contrasts of red-berried rowan trees along the roadsides, to the pale green of birch woodlands down a hill slope on a spring morning. In late summer, the mauve of great sweeps of heather against the deep green of ancient pinewoods in Speyside and Deeside presents a landscape unique in Europe.

Human influence on this landscape can readily be seen in the pattern of farming, from the great arable acres of the coastal lowlands to the tiny crofts of the north-west, as well as the small burghs which are such a characteristic feature of much of Scotland. In the north-west Highlands, there are still vast tracts of upland country without roads, other than hill tracks, but it is not generally known that some of the remotest country with least human habitation is in the green hills of the Borders. Visitors often remark on the pleasure of motoring on roads relatively free from traffic, and the abundance of unspoilt countryside for walking.

On access to this countryside, Scotland has some distinctive features. While it is often claimed that there is no law of trespass in Scotland, the strictly legal situation is little different from that elsewhere in Britain; it is not an offence simply to be on private land, although this does not extend to camping or the lighting of fires. There is a long-standing tradition of public access on open hill land provided that no damage or disturbance is created, although sporting estates are increasingly discouraging access during the deer stalking season. The right to roam, as it is known, is fiercely defended by walking and climbing associations, but the same groups are often equally resistant to the formal development in remote areas of public access facilities, including way-marking, bridge construction, designation of long-distance footpaths and so on, to protect their wilderness quality. The resulting compromise means that although visitors have access to the countryside, they seldom know exactly where to go; walkers going into the hills are required to find their own way, armed with map and compass. Fortunately, there are now a number of good guide books available for the better-known routes.

Although legal rights of way are much less common in Scotland than in England, a number of authorities and organisations have provided access to their land or to private land by agreement with owners, notably the Forestry Commission and local authorities - especially in Country Parks in the vicinity of population centres - and several voluntary conservation organisations such as the National Trust for Scotland and Scottish Wildlife Trust. Scottish Natural Heritage and other agencies have designated long-distance footpaths, often using old droving routes, such as the path through the Lairig Ghru in the Cairngorms, while most tourist information centres can provide guidance on local walks. There is a general rule that in areas with domestic stock, dogs should be kept on a lead. Unfortunately, visitors do not always appreciate how extreme and variable conditions can be in the Scottish mountains even at the height of summer, and that, notwithstanding modest altitudes, the environment must be treated with considerable respect. Walkers are strongly advised to be prepared for any weather, to wear strong waterproof footwear, and to carry food and emergency supplies.

Mountains

The mountains are extatic and ought to be visited in pilgrimage once a year.

Thomas Gray, – *letter to William Mason,* 2 November 1765

Of all the landscapes of Scotland, it is the mountain scenery which dominates the view – mountains which are usually referred to locally as 'hills'. Despite extensive afforestation, these hills and moorlands are still treeless over large areas. This open country, characterised by heather moorland and upland grassland, has been changed over the centuries by grazing stock and burning – the heather moors, maintained by fire, are unlike any other landscape in Europe. Where richer mineral soils occur in the mountains, and grazing is absent, rare arctic-alpine plants are found, often at much lower altitudes than their counterparts in Continental Europe. In terms of ecological change, walking up Ben Nevis is equivalent to travelling a thousand miles north of Scotland, to find the equivalent sub-arctic conditions and species. In another dimension, it is comparable to travelling back 10,000 years in time when, emerging from the great melting ice sheets, virtually the whole of the country would have had a similar appearance to that of the summits of our highest mountains today.

The upland areas of Scotland are important for their populations of such predatory birds as peregrine falcon and golden eagle which have their European strongholds here. Above the tree line, conditions are similar to those of the sub-arctic tundra, with species such as the mountain hare, the snow bunting and the ptarmigan, all startling white in winter. Vegetation on the higher summits can be reduced to a few mosses and lichens among a semi-desert of rock and bare soil, sorted into geometric patterns by frost action. This is the last large area of wilderness in the country and has special value, not only for northern wildlife in spectacular scenery, but also for active recreation by walkers, climbers and skiers.

The extensive deep blanket peats of Scotland's northern regions result mainly from the cool, moist climate in this zone. They have their own very specialised plants and insects, notably a wide range of sphagnum mosses which thrive in cool, moist conditions, usually where the waters are naturally acid. The area is also important for a number of wading birds which breed on these peaty wetlands, including golden plover, dunlin, greenshank and curlew, while the open pools and small lochans are sanctuaries for both the red-throated and the rare black-throated divers, all species of the sub-arctic.

A distinctive feature of the Scottish mountains is the depression of the tree line, usually below 500m/1,500ft, mainly due to exposure. There are very few examples of the natural tree line with stunted trees and scrub that characterises mountain landscapes elsewhere in Europe; it is replaced by dwarf shrubs and grassland which can resist both exposure and the grazing pressures prevalent on Scottish hills. Often the dwarf shrub is of heathers, blaeberry (bilberry), cowberry and crowberry, with abundant mosses and grey or yellow lichens giving rock surfaces their distinctive colours. Any isolated trees that occur will be pines or, more frequently, birch or rowan. Rowan seeds are often dispersed by birds a considerable distance from the mother tree, while birch produces innumerable small, wind-blown seeds. It is frequently the first tree pioneer on drier areas, while scrub willow colonises the wetter hollows. In north-facing corries, snow may lie in small patches throughout the year, and here blaeberry will replace the heather which cannot tolerate long snow cover. Some of the mountain plants in these cold slopes grow for only a few weeks between August and September. Where the snow melts by July, sub-alpine grassland may dominate, with the pink moss campion on the plateaus and gentler slopes.

Most of the mountain soils are derived from acid rocks, breaking down in the granite areas to sandy, gravelly soils which encourage heather growth in the drier areas, especially in the east of the country. The first heather to appear in July with its deep purple flowers is the bell heather, followed by the ling in August. These species are crucial to the red grouse, which feeds on young shoots and seeds and uses the vegetation for cover from predators. A hectare of good moorland will support one breeding pair, but this can fall to one pair per 20-40 hectares/50-100 acres on the poorest ground in the west of the country. Meadow pipits and wheatears are also common where the heather is thickest.

On wetter peaty ground, the heather is replaced by sphagnum mosses, bog asphodel, the fragrant bog myrtle and deer sedge, attractive to stonechats and whinchats. In the west, where open pools also occur, this is the haunt of snipe and greenshank, with curlew favouring areas of taller grass. On the driest gravelly soils, the dark green leathery leaves of the bearberry make their appearance on the high moorland, often with cowberry. Where the ground is richer, non-woody plants become more frequent and include thyme and violets in fescue grassland. Lime-rich soils with sufficient moisture produce the showy yellow saxifrage.

The symbolic bird of the mountains is undoubtedly the golden eagle, with its characteristic long gliding flight quartering the ridges, often disappearing tantalisingly over the far slope. In the west of the country, the eagle typically feeds on deer and sheep carrion, and the extensive use of toxic sheep dips caused a marked decline in its numbers in that area during the 1960s, whereas the greater availability of grouse, ptarmigan and hare on the eastern moorlands contributes to breeding success. With the ban on certain chemicals, numbers have risen throughout the country, so that Scotland now has the strongest population of the species in Europe. Unfortunately the bird is still persecuted particularly on the grouse moors of the east, in common with other predators such as the hen harrier.

One species which has declined progressively over a long period, to the point of virtual extinction in the west, is the black grouse, with its highly distinctive plumage and aggressive mating displays on the 'lek' – the open glades between forest and moorland. The burning and severe grazing of this forest margin have almost certainly caused the decline of this attractive game bird throughout the country. A more truly mountain bird is the ptarmigan, rarely found below 650m/2,000ft, which feeds on blaeberry and crowberry shoots. Extremely difficult to detect in summer with its mottled plumage against a background of rocks, and with its white camouflage in winter, it is probably one of the hardiest birds in the world, capable of overnighting in a shallow snow-scrape on the highest ridges.

Of all the mountain areas of Britain, the Cairngorm plateau in the Central Highlands has the largest extent and range of montane habitats, including the highest and most extensive blanket peat bogs. It also represents the most arctic climate in the country, with the greatest area of permanent snow in its north-facing corries. Here are found impressive glacial features of ice lochs and ice-scoured glens and cliffs, with a huge summit plateau supporting tundra-type vegetation and typical arctic plant and animal communities, such as trailing azalea, arctic chickweed, dwarf willow and highland saxifrage; about 30 per cent of the unique British mountain flora is found here. The frost-shattered rocks and soils at the highest altitudes are almost unvegetated and there are extensive bare boulder fields and granite screes. Of the nesting arctic birds, the concentration of ptarmigan and dotterel is higher here than anywhere else in the world, with high populations also of the snow bunting. It is not surprising that with this wealth of interest, which includes extensive native pinewood, heather moorland and montane wetlands, the whole area (currently a National Nature Reserve) is a proposed World Heritage Site.

In contrast to the predominantly poor acid rocks of the Cairngorms, the Breadalbane range in north Perthshire has a higher proportion of lime-rich outcrops, especially on the crumbling gravelly schists of Ben Lawers, rising to 1,214m/3,984ft. Here the combination of high altitude and relatively rich soils provides just the right conditions for probably the best range of arctic-alpine plant communities in Britain, including the bright blue alpine gentian, the extremely rare alpine forget-me-not, and the daisy-like purple flowers of the alpine fleabane. There are some 75 different species of montane plants, mainly concentrated on the cliff ledges and faces of this remarkable mountain, which also supports late snow-bed vegetation and mountain bog communities. There is also a rich mollusc fauna, including a number of lowland species found here at unusually high altitudes, and upland butterflies such as the mountain ringlet. The ecology and land use of this National Nature Reserve is well presented in the National Trust for Scotland's mountain visitor centre and nature trail.

The geology and climate of both these areas are in marked contrast to those of the mountains of the north-west Highlands, typified by Beinn Eighe in the Torridon district of Wester Ross. The base rock of the ancient Lewisian gneiss, up to 1,600 million years old, is overlain by the later Torridonian sandstones and the relatively young Cambrian quartzites of a mere 600 million years ago. From the evidence of pollen preserved in local peat, it is known that this area saw the first colonisation by birch and native Scots pinewood over 8,000 years ago, after the last Ice Age. Here the mountain trail climbs through different zones of climate, vegetation and wildlife: every 305m/1,000ft of this trail represents a distance of 965km/600miles northwards towards the Arctic, from the relatively luxuriant deep pinewood to the barren rocks of the summit area. The area, declared as the first National Nature Reserve in Britain, covers a typical range of habitats of highland Scotland in a very dramatic setting of woodland, loch and mountain.

The trail initially follows the Alt na h-Airidhe burn, the 'stream of the shieling' (or summer grazing), which has cut a spectacular gorge through a fault line further up in its course. The route then winds through a very fine fragment of the old Caledonian pinewood called Coille na Glas Leitire ('wood of the grey slope') which at one time must have harboured many of the animals referred to above - boar, elk, bear, wolf - all now vanished as their habitat contracted. Now the forest provides shelter for both red and roe deer, as well as wildcat, pine marten and red squirrel. Birds include the Scottish crossbill, feeding entirely on pine seed, and now confined to Scotland with a population of about 500 pairs. At 150m/450ft the track becomes steeper and crosses a typical area of wet mountain bog without trees, but with specialised plant and animal life, dominated by sphagnum mosses.

Above the bog, there are spectacular views across the great mountain mass of Slioch, demonstrating the ancient geology of the area, and the beautiful Loch Maree, with black-throated divers, red-breasted mergansers and goosanders all feeding on its rich fishery of salmon, sea trout, brown trout and char. The islands of Loch Maree, in their plentiful regeneration of pine-wood, show very clearly the effects of protection from grazing animals. At 300m/1,000ft, the few pine trees have become dwarfed and wind-sculpted, and most of the vegetation is dominated by heather supporting a few red grouse. Among the heather may be found the dwarf cornel, a plant of the Arctic, with its distinctive black flowers against their white petals.

From the plateau at 550m/1,650ft more than 30 tops over 915m/3,000ft can be seen on a good day. Here plant life is particularly sparse and adapted to the harsh conditions, mainly low-growing shrubs such as prostrate juniper, mountain azalea, crowberry and alpine bearberry. Deer grass and clubmosses are common, together with various mountain sedges. This vegetation is comparable to the arctic tundra 1,600km/1,000miles further north, with many of the plants under snow for 5 months or more in the year. The plateau loch, despite its altitude, supports frogs and large numbers of palmate newt, as well as caddis flies, and common hawker dragonflies. Around the loch is typical ptarmigan and mountain hare country, and the open treeless terrain is good hunting ground for golden eagle and raven. Taken together, the mountain zones that can be seen from this trail over its altitudinal range give a very typical picture of the hill country ecology of the north-west Highlands.

Woodlands

Ettrick Foreste is a fair foreste, in it grows many a seemly tree,
There's hart and hind and deer and roe,
And of a' wild bestis grete plentie.

Ballad of the Outlaw Murray

The natural vegetation of Scotland, at least up to the middle hill slopes, would be woodland, were it not for man's activities. There is good evidence from pollen remains and portions of trees buried in peat that tree cover was not only much more extensive at one time, but could also be found at much higher altitudes than today. Forests apparently survived even in the interglacial period, containing such conifers as Norway spruce and silver fir, which are not now considered native tree species. There appears to have been a particularly favourable climate for woodland about 7,000 years ago, when the forest reached its maximum extent. The indications are that this was mainly deciduous, although pine appears to have later replaced the broadleaves on the drier sites. The broadleaf woodland supported a wide range of tree and shrub species, including oak, ash, birch, elm, lime, bird cherry, aspen, alder, willows, holly and hazel. The upper tree line in the hills was more scrub than woodland, mainly hazel, birch, rowan and juniper.

This would have been a forest of considerable variety, with many open glades, bogs and patches of dense scrub supporting a rich fauna, including many of the larger mammals which have now become extinct in Scotland. Different species of deer, for example, were known to the early settlers and there are written references in the old Gaelic poems to elk, reindeer and wolves, several of which also appear on the sculptured stones of the Picts. The wolves were sufficiently numerous to be a considerable menace to medieval stock farmers and there are frequent references ('noisum to tame bestiale') to their attacks on domestic animals. Burial sites on islands and the use of heavy slab gravestones were devices to thwart grave-robbing by wolves, who survived in Scotland into the mid-19th century, despite the generous bounty placed on their heads.

Climatic changes within historic times helped the spread of peat and considerably reduced the extent and nature of the forest cover, with different species such as elm, birch and hazel becoming more frequent at different times. Even on the remote and now treeless St Kilda, the remains of birch and hazel scrub have been found. Cereal grains start appearing in later peat layers, and their increase clearly indicates how the forest was progressively cleared for farming, especially in the Neolithic period. The name 'Caledonia' given by the Romans to Scotland means 'the woods on the heights', and other place names from the Borders to the far north indicate that substantial tracts of forest remained at this time: Ettrick, Jedwood and Galloway Forests, Torwood in central Scotland, and Alyth, Cabrach and Buchan Forests further north. Forest clearance continued down the centuries to the point where travellers such as Samuel Johnson were commenting specifically on Scotland's treeless state in the late 18th century, and in 1771 Thomas Pennant, travelling through the Blair Atholl district, declared: 'This country is very mountainous and has no natural woods except birch, but the vast plantations which begin to cloathe the hills will amply supply these deficits.'

Many trees were planted around this time by landowners, especially in Perthshire, using the seeds of new conifer species brought back from North America and beautifying their estates with introductions such as beech, sycamore and chestnut. The availability of cheap timber from the Baltic countries in the 19th century did not however encourage large-scale domestic afforestation. The lowest extent of woodland in Scotland was probably in the latter half of the 19th century, when it was estimated that only 297,364ha/734,490 acres of woodland remained.

Truly native deciduous woodland is now extremely scarce and is often confined to steepsided gorges unsuitable for cultivation, where even grazing stock could not reach. They remain important habitats for woodland animals such as badger, and birds such as pied flycatcher and green woodpecker. Many of these remnants are in a precarious state because they are small and fragmented, with little natural regeneration. The most extensive broadleaf woods are in the west, especially Argyll, where the cool, moist climate has encouraged the growth of native oakwoods, carpeted with mosses and ferns, which thrive under damp, shady conditions. These include the quaintly named hay-scented buckler fern, filmy fern, hard fern and common polypody, along with the very many non-flowering plants which characterise these damp acid woodlands, covering trees and rocks alike. There are about 236 species of ground plants (excluding trees and shrubs) associated with native woodland, of which about 70-80, because of their particular requirements, are exclusive to such woods.

Most of the accessible woodlands were extensively coppiced for charcoal, required for smelting iron in earlier times, or managed for bark used in leather-tanning processes. Many of these are now extremely attractive open woods, with a variety of light and shade which provides the right conditions for many different woodland flower species including dog's mercury, wood anemone, primrose, dog violet, wild garlic and wild hyacinth, all of which make sheets of colour in springtime, when these woods are at their best. Elsewhere, as in the Clyde Valley, the woods are mixed with elm and ash on richer soils over an understorey of hazel, in narrow, steeply sloping side valleys. Unfortunately many of these woodlands, especially in the west, have been invaded by rhododendron, introduced as a feature in estate grounds, which is in some cases spreading out of control to the detriment of many native shrubs and tree species.

A good example of a protected native broadleaf woodland can be found within the National Nature Reserve of Loch Lomond on the island of Inchcailloch, immediately offshore from Balmaha on the eastern shore of the loch. The island has the added interest of lying across the Highland Boundary Fault, displaying a variety of rock types and soils which produce very different types of wood-land. From the top of this island, there are magnificent views of the two faces of Scotland: looking north up the loch its steeply sloping shores merge into typical Highland scenery with an impressive mountain backdrop, while to the south the River Endrick meanders gently through lowlands and the rich agricultural country around the western end of the Carse of Stirling.

The island itself is said to take its name ('island of the old women') from the 12th century nunnery, and the remains of the old church and graveyard are still visible. There is no doubt that the woodland has been considerably modified since earliest times, but it is still a good example of a typical mossy western oakwood, coppiced for charcoal and tan bark from the second half of the 17th century, as were so many woods in this district, alongside their use for wood distillates: there was a small pyroligneous acid (wood-spirit) factory near Balmaha in the 19th century. One result of this commercial forestry activity was the removal of non-productive or 'barren' timber such as ash, elm and alder, to create almost pure stands of oak. Coupled with subsequent sheep grazing and oak planting, many of these Loch Lomond woodlands had their natural structure quite markedly altered.

Although the soils are mainly acid under the oakwood (which is replaced by Scots pine over heather near the summit) there are richer patches which support ash and, along the shore, alder, willow, bog myrtle, broom, gorse and guelder rose. In open, drier areas both ling and bell heather form small heathy patches with blaeberry in the more shaded slopes. In the centre of the island, hazel becomes more frequent than holly as the main shrub under oak and birch, and ground flora is dominated by greater woodrush, male fern, bramble and Yorkshire fog. Inchcailloch supports many woodland bird species, among them wood warbler, chiffchaff, woodcock, long-tailed tit, tawny owl and redstart – a total summer population of over 34 species of birds, including an exceptional density of wrens. This great range is probably due partly to the history of woodland management which has created an unusually wide range of habitats, making the much-used nature trail very attractive to visitors.

A very different woodland type can be found on another of the loch's islands, Inchlonaig, which boasts one of the very few yew woods in Scotland. Some of these ancient scattered trees exceed

300cm/118in in diameter, and according to legend were planted by Robert the Bruce for supplying his bowmen. In the mid-17th century a deer park was created here (its fallow deer are now well known), and many of the deer introduced have spread to other islands and the mainland. Other examples comprising almost pure woodlands of native species include the extensive alder wood at the Mound at the head of Loch Fleet in Sutherland, occupying the sediments of the delta there, and the birch wood of Craigellachie on the craggy slopes above Aviemore. Here there are both the silver birch typical of eastern Scotland and the downy birch commoner on the schist rocks of the west. Although the birch wood at first sight seems unvaried, there are scattered rowan, aspen, oak, wych elm, hazel and bird cherry over a ground cover of grasses and mosses. Previously grazed by sheep, the woodland is now much used by wintering red deer, which almost certainly keeps it open and may help to maintain favourable conditions for the many species of localised moths for which the wood is famed, including eagle striped sallow, Kentish glory and Rannoch sprawler. Buzzard are common circling over the scrub-covered cliffs, which also support a consistently successful peregrine breeding site, despite heavy traffic on the trunk road nearby.

Our only native coniferous tree, the Scots pine, dominates the relicts of the once great Caledonian Forest of the Highlands, best represented in Deeside, Speyside, and the glens west of Inverness such as Strathfarrar and Glen Affric. The pinewood of Scotland is probably the largest continuous area of native forest in the whole of Britain, and a stroll through some of the older forest can be an inspiring experience: great gnarled 'granny' pines, perhaps in excess of 300 years old, littering the forest floor with their prolific woody cones. Part of the attraction of these scented woodlands is the variety of shape and form of the salmon-pink trunks of the pine, interspersed with equally varied juniper, from stunted and deer-browsed bushes to almost perfect green cones, rising over 5m/15ft beneath the pinewood canopy. This is not the impenetrable darkness of a modern spruce plantation, but an inviting mosaic of light and shade created by trees of different size, age and spacing, sometimes opening out into purple heathland or the surprise of an emerald bed of sphagnum. Here and there, clumps of birch and scattered rowan vary the pattern, with dense carpets of blaeberry underneath. My first encounter with the Rothiemurchus woods at the end of a long trek through the Lairig Ghru, as a sixteen year-old, was an experience which left a deep and lasting impression.

Out on the moorland, beyond the forest proper, scattered and isolated ancient pine trees have been twisted by the wind into fantastic shapes, and where grazing is not too severe, their progeny can be seen pushing up above the heather on the leeward side. Although these heavily branching trees may look natural, they are however often the relicts of old fellings which have removed all the best and straightest timber, since there are probably no pine forests which have not been felled at one time or another – we know for example that massive quantities of timber were floated down the Spey in earlier centuries from the great pinewoods of this district. With the incursion of sheep in the 18th and 19th centuries many of these woods began to die, and in a number of cases it was wartime timber extraction which sufficiently disturbed the soil surface to provide conditions for pine seed germination.

Although Scots pine appears by its name to be specific to Scotland, it is one of the most widespread of tree species, extending to the east Pacific Coast and surviving in a wide variety of situations. Its deep tap root enables it to cope with dry conditions, and it predominates on the well-drained granite soils of north-eastern Scotland, often growing to a considerable age and reaching heights in excess of 50m/150ft. In wetter peaty areas it gives way to birch, which as a pioneer may help to dry out such boggy sites, enabling the pine to colonise from the margins and eventually change wetland into woodland. It produces high-quality timber when carefully managed, but unfortunately is slow-growing compared to such introduced species as sitka spruce, which has the additional advantage of being able to tolerate wet peaty conditions. These species introduced from the West Pacific have largely replaced the native pine in large-scale plantings since World War II, and only relatively recently has serious attention been given to the conservation and protection of our remaining Caledonian pinewood through special incentive schemes for private landowners.

One good reason for special conservation measures is that the native Scots pinewood is intimately associated with the Highland scene and its wildlife. It provides sanctuary for such characteristic Scottish species as pine marten, wildcat, red squirrel, capercailzie and the unique Scottish crossbill. The first of these often has its den in cairns or holes in old trees, but it has been known to nest in old eagle eyries. A weasel-like creature about 0.8m/2.5ft long with a distinctive creamy white or orange throat contrasting with its mainly dark chestnut colour, it feeds on small rodents or birds, which in times past made it a target of the gamekeeper. Now it is spreading from the north-west into the new territories created by modern forestry plantations where it is not discouraged. By contrast, the capercailzie hunted to extinction in the late 18th century before being reintroduced, appears to be declining, from 20,000 in the mid 1970's to a mere 2,200 in 1996. This spectacular pinewood bird, (which can be heavier than a golden eagle) is the largest member of the grouse family, but has lost much of its original open pinewood habitat and has been overshot. Like the black grouse, it has a distinctive mating display on its 'lekking' ground, usually a pinewood clearing, spreading its fan tail, puffing out its chest, and extending its head aggressively forward to impress both rivals and any watching female.

A readily accessible example of a native pinewood can be seen at Glen Tanar near Aboyne in Deeside. The coarse sandy and gravelly drift soils, left behind by the glacier that swept down this valley, form typical granitic Highland soils on which the pinewood thrives. Although there has been much planting of pine, there are still fine relicts of the ancient pinewood along the Tanar river, with a few birch and juniper. Glen Tanar is noted for some huge old pine trees, with woodland extending up heathery slopes mixed with a rich variety of mosses. The visitor can see the characteristic but often quite inconspicuous pine wood flowers – twayblade, creeping lady's tresses and several species of wintergreen. Easier to recognise may be a wood ants' nest as a conical heap of dried pine needles, heaving with the activity of the black ants. Crested tits which are entirely confined to pinewood can be heard, and the crossbill may make its presence felt by showering the visitor from above with pine shoots, severed by its secateur-like beak. The public trail leading through the pinewood is extended over the moorland where crowberry and cloudberry can be found among the heather and mosses.

Now that sheep have been removed from many of the surrounding areas, one of the main threats to the survival of the pinewood is from red deer whose numbers in recent years, aided by a run of mild winters, have reached record levels. Deer fencing is expensive, but the heavy culls of hinds required to bring numbers down rapidly is difficult to achieve by traditional stalking techniques with the reduced manpower on modern estates. A hard winter can result in heavy mortality from slow starvation, especially of younger and weaker beasts.

Coast

The Atlantic surge
Pours in among the stormy Hebridies

James Thomson 'Autumn', The Seasons (1730)

For a country of its size, Scotland has an astonishingly varied coastline, ranging from high sand dunes to shingle, from some of the tallest sea cliffs in Europe to expanses of intertidal estuarine mud and saltmarsh. Away from the industrialised estuaries, the coast is probably the least altered of all its environments, especially the remoter rock cliffs and islands, from St Kilda in the far west to the coastal cliffs of Berwickshire. Together with Orkney, Shetland and the coasts of Caithness and Aberdeenshire, with isolated islands such as Ailsa Craig in the Firth of Clyde and the Bass Rock in the Forth, these are home to literally millions of colonial sea birds which here make up a high proportion of the world's population of particular species. They include razorbills, gannets, skuas, puffins and kittiwakes, providing a wildlife spectacle during the nesting season. Of at least equal international importance are the Scottish estuaries and salt marshes, which support many thousands of wintering migratory wildfowl, notably the Inner Solway, the Moray Firth, the Tay, and those of the island of Islay. These include barnacle and Greenland white-fronted geese, golden eye, scaup and great crested grebes in numbers of global significance.

Associated with the west coast are the sand dunes and dune grasslands known by the Gaelic name, *machair*. These windswept grasslands are formed from lime-rich shell sands and enriched by seaweed as local fertiliser; they are either grazed or lightly cultivated. Because chemicals are not usually applied, these sea-meadows, especially in the Outer Hebrides, burst into bloom in the spring and early summer with a profusion of meadow flowers that have disappeared from many other farmed areas on the mainland. They also provide a unique habitat for many species of ground-nesting birds, such as skylark, lapwing and oyster catcher.

In this account, a few sites have been selected from each of the coastal regions to represent different coastal landscapes, from rocky cliffs and islands to estuaries and sand dunes.

South-west Scotland, between the high cliffs of the Mull of Galloway overlooking the Irish Sea and the great expanses of estuarine mud in the inner Solway Firth, has some of the most varied coastline in Britain, fortunately unspoiled for the most part. This coast is characterised by long sandy estuaries behind which lie pastoral landscapes not unlike those of south-west England and southern Ireland. A little further inland towards Newton Stewart in the west, the coast is backed by impressive mountain landscapes formed by the great granite bosses of the Cairnsmore of Fleet and the Merrick. Facing southwards beneath this sheltering arc of mountains, the coast has an especially mild and sunny climate which attracts increasing numbers of visitors. The shape of the coast is highly distinctive, with the protruding peninsulas of the Rhinns of Galloway in the far west and the Machars of Wigtown enclosing the great stretches of sand and salt marshes around Luce Bay. Another unusual feature of this coast, particularly west of Kircudbright, is the wind-pruned coastal scrub woodland which clings to the cliff face below the raised beaches of the middle Solway.

Stretching for almost 10km/6 miles between the Rivers Nith and Lochar at the extreme eastern end of the Solway Firth at Caerlaverock is one of the most extensive areas of salt marsh and mud flats in Britain. Lying on a high tilted shore, this area is subject to massive movement of its muds and sands, so that the shoreline and network of channels and creeks is constantly changing. Here sea-meadow grass has colonised the exposed sand to build up mounds which are then invaded by thrift, sea aster and sea lavender, making the 'merse' such a colourful sight in late spring and early summer.

Offshore, the great expanses of mudflats and sands appear monotonous but, washed daily by the tides, they are home to vast numbers of tiny marine animals and algae which provide rich feeding for the great flocks of wildfowl and waders using this area, especially in winter. The numbers of knot and black-tailed godwit are among the highest in Britain, and it has good populations of redshank and shelduck This National Nature Reserve is however noted mainly for its overwintering geese flocks, especially the barnacle goose which migrates annually in thousands from Spitzbergen in the Arctic. Many of the wildfowl that congregate here can be easily seen from the viewing hides and towers which the Wildfowl and Wetland Trust have constructed around the margin of the merse. For those whose interest is historical, the impressive red sandstone Caerlaverock Castle, with its surrounding moat and surprising Renaissance architecture in the interior courtyard, is well worth a visit.

The south-eastern coast down to the border with England includes some of the finest coastal cliff scenery in Britain and towards the Firth of Forth displays a variety of coastal landscapes from salt marsh to impressive sweeps of sandy beach between North Berwick and Gullane. In between, a wide outcropping Carboniferous limestone reef near Dunbar provides the raw material for the local cement industry. John Muir, the renowned conservationist and founder of the National Parks movement in the United States, was born near here and is commemorated in the John Muir Country Park which covers the estuary of the River Tyne and the immediate coastlands, backed by the fine woods and rich arable farmland of the Tynninghame Estate. One of the most spectacular sights anywhere along the Scottish coast is the great white volcanic mass of the Bass Rock, its colour the result of the droppings of many thousands of gannets (whose Latin name *Sula bassana* comes from this famous breeding site) which can be visited by regular boat trips from North Berwick. Immediately west of this small coastal town, Tantallon Castle, a magnificent early medieval ruin, made full use of the high volcanic cliffs to establish a position virtually impregnable from the sea. Visitors have the added bonus of seeing nesting kittiwakes within a few yards of its great curtain wall.

Of all the landscapes on this stretch of coast, the most dramatic is provided by the great felsite mass of the cliffs around St Abb's Head, a few miles north of Eyemouth. This is a wild coast of gullies and coves, of reefs and skerries and 152m/500ft cliffs hanging sheer above the crashing waves at their foot. Added drama is provided by the gaunt ruin of the 14th century Fast Castle, perched 21m/170ft above the sea. The cliffs and their hinterland are jointly managed as a reserve by the National Trust for Scotland and the Scottish Wildlife Trust, and provide a sanctuary for thousands of nesting seabirds, including kittiwakes, guillemots and razorbills - in the breeding season, the sound of their cries and almost melancholy sighing against a background of waves beating against the red rocks is a memorable experience. This is also the season to view the sheets of purple thrift which dominate the cliff tops. St Abbs itself, a quiet fishing settlement, is the centre of one of Britain's foremost diving areas, taking advantage of the rich and varied sea life to be found in these exceptionally clear waters, now designated as a voluntary marine reserve for this reason.

The north-east coast is conveniently divided into the shores bordering the Moray Firth, with its neat little fishing villages tucked into sheltered coves – there are some 70 such villages along this 24Lkm/150miles stretch – and the mainly sandy coast of the North Sea extending from Aberdeen northwards. Near the western extremity of this coastal region, close to the village of Findhorn, lies what must at one time have been the finest and most extensive tract of sand dunes in the whole of Britain at Culbin Sands, stretching for over 11km/7miles. Here the dunes reach 30m/100ft in height in a series of long ridges which can still be discerned today, despite the vast tract of plantation forestry, covering over 2,000ha/5,000 acres, now masking the original sand hills. The dunes themselves hide a whole estate and settlement which in the late 17th century became overwhelmed by sand, thought to have been the result of large-scale removal of the dune marram grass for roof thatching. Special features of this area are the long shingle bars underlying the sand, which surface periodically within the dark forest, and support a distinctive lichen flora.

North of Collieston, the Dalradian schists of the great Buchan plateau form cliffs and sea stacks in an exciting sea landscape which includes the pink granites south of Peterhead. In this area there is a huge rock cauldron, the Bullers of Buchan, almost 50m/150ft in depth, which extends out into the open sea through an awesome arch in the great granite cliffs. On stormy days the sea spouts dramatically through this cauldron, a demonstration of the erosive power which has exploited the weaknesses in the rock joints to create such spectacles. The cauldron is readily accessible from the main A975 road from Aberdeen. A similar blow hole occurs at Hell's Lum near Pennan on the Moray coast.

From the Dee estuary northwards, there is an almost unbroken line of wide sandy foreshore and dunes for over 19km/12miles, as far as the Ythan Estuary near Newburgh. This marks the southern boundary of a remarkable sand dune system, frequently described

as a 'miniature Sahara', known as the Sands of Forvie. The summit of the highest dune reaches 57m/187ft above-sea level in a
wilderness of shifting sand covering the National Nature Reserve,
which has for many years also been an important site for research
into coastal ecology, especially wildfowl behaviour, from the nearby University of Aberdeen research station. These huge sand hills
reach northwards to the outskirts of Collieston, and from time to
time gales disturb vast quantities of sand, sometimes uncovering
evidence of prehistoric human settlements of both Bronze and Iron
Ages. On the landward side, the mobile dunes are replaced by
dune grassland, often with much lichen, while further inland still,
by dune heath and wet hollows known as 'slacks'.

This reserve supports the largest concentration of eider duck
in Britain and has important colonies of terns, kittiwakes, fulmars,
shelduck and oystercatchers. The eider are concentrated round the
estuary of the River Ythan, with peak winter numbers of almost
1,000 birds, rising to over 4,500 in summer. Eiders are notable for
forming creches of young birds from different broods, cared for by
several adults rotating their duties – a common sight around the
Scottish coast in late spring is such a creche paddling in a tight
excitable mass behind more sedate female birds, usually in the
comparative shelter of inlets and coves. At the Sands of Forvie it
has been found that 80 per cent of mortality among young birds
is due to predation by large gulls, with much higher mortality in
bad weather, when the young can become separated from the par-
ent birds.

The north-west coast is the nearest landscape in Scotland to
the fjord scenery of Norway, characterised by deep sea lochs penetrating far inland, into country distinguished by its barren mountains, bare rock and treeless moors and bogs. Much of it takes the
full brunt of the Atlantic storms, and the sense of wilderness is
enhanced by the ancient grey-and pink rocks, the oldest being the
Lewisian gneiss already referred to. Some of this coast is extremely remote and cannot be accessed by road; these are among the
wildest shores in Britain, quite uninhabited over considerable
areas. The main A838 road from the north coast along the
Pentland Firth avoids the most north-westerly point of Cape
Wrath, but good views of this unique area can be had south of
Rhiconich, especially if a detour is taken along the switch-back
B869 towards the Point of Stoer. Between the outcrops of ancient

foreland rocks occur some of the finest stretches of sandy beach anywhere in the country, such as Oldshoremore, made all the more attractive by their mountain backdrop. Here the lime-rich machair with its show of summer flowers makes its appearance, a low series of grassy dunes behind the beach.

From the A894 the tiny settlement of Tarbet can be reached just south of Loch Laxford, with the fantastic, sculpted topography of an almost lunar landscape. From Tarbet a regular summer boat service runs to Handa Island, a bird reserve managed by the Scottish Wildlife Trust. This island, measuring about 306ha/766 acres, has fearsome 122m/400ft sheer sandstone cliffs at its northern end, sloping to the south where the island presents a gentler face of sandy beaches and reefs. The warm red rocks of Torridonian sandstone on Handa are in marked contrast to the cold grey of the surrounding Lewisian gneiss across the Sound of Handa on the mainland.

From the northern end of the trail across the island, it is possible to look down the precipitous 'geo', or rock chasm, some 91m/300ft and view the Great Stack, a massive sandstone pillar. Here the birds are layered on the ledges as if in some ornithological high-rise flats, full of tightly packed auks, easily seen from the adjacent headlands which almost encircle the stack. Some of the finest views of the mountainous north-west mainland can be seen from here on a clear day. The bird hunters of Lewis are reputed to have raided the stack by stretching a long home-made rope between the headlands, suspended 107m/350ft above the sea, from which they dropped on to the stack to collect eggs and young birds. There is considerable historic interest in the early communities of the island, which like those on St Kilda succeeded in surviving on potatoes, seafood, seabirds and their eggs. They were driven to emigration by the potato famine of the mid-19th century and remains of the croft houses, fields and old graveyard can still be seen. Now the island is home to vast congregations of seabirds, including guillemots, kittiwakes, fulmars, shags and herring gulls, and has been colonised by the great skua in recent times – there are more birds here than on the Bass Rock and Ailsa Craig put together.

The west coast of Scotland south of the Firth of Lorne has an altogether gentler and softer appearance than the rugged northwest, and the milder climate encourages lusher vegetation and impressive coastal woodlands, such as those at Mealdarroch,

south of Skipness on the Kintyre Peninsula. There are many sheltered waters along the great sea lochs which provide welcome
havens for yachts and in many areas it is still more convenient to
cross water than land, as the roads have to make lengthy circum-
navigations of the sea arms which cut into this country. One of
these, Loch Sween, leading into the Sound of Jura, some
60km/37miles south of Oban, is an especially good example of a
south-western sea loch, recently proposed as Scotland's first
marine nature reserve. It extends for 14km/9miles inland with a
very complex shape, forming hidden sheltered arms which create
great ecological variety. The loch has a particularly rich marine
life, including clams, sea urchins, various types of starfish,
sponges, sea anemones and beautiful coral-like seaweed beds
known as maerl. The exceptionally small tidal rise and fall of the
loch, less than 1m/3ft, in this very sheltered situation creates a pro-
nounced horizontal zonation of the various marine plants and animals. Otters and common seals are plentiful, and on the islands
there is a wide range of sea birds, with especially large colonies
of shags as well as breeding common terns. Not surprisingly, this
is a favourite area for divers and underwater photographers
attracted by the sheer variety of underwater wildlife in an incomparable setting of wooded islands and peninsulas. The proposed
legal protection of this outstanding area, however, is still a matter
of considerable local controversy, with the local community chal-
lenging the need for any additional controls which they anticipate
would follow from statutory designation.

Lochs and Rivers

*The superb Loch Lomond ... I shall often dream of Tarbet,
even in the midst of lovely Italy with its oranges, its myr-
tles, its laurels, and its jessamines.*

B Faujas St Fond – *Travels in England and Scotland* (1784)

' By Tummel and Loch Rannoch and Lochaber I must go . . .' goes
the song, celebrating the glory of routes through the glens of the
Highland scene. Scotland has a high proportion of the total area
of fresh water in Britain: although in Britain as a whole fresh

water covers only 1 per cent of the land area, in the Highlands and islands this rises to 5 per cent and in areas such as the Western Isles to 10 per cent, largely as a result of past glaciation, with hard underlying rocks holding much of the high rainfall. In the north and west the waters tend to be deeper, low in organic content, and clear, while the softer rocks of the south produce shallower, nutrient-rich lochs. The deep lochs found in glaciated valleys and those formed in the small mountain corries are a particular feature of the Scottish Highlands, although similar to those in Norway and the European Alps. The innumerable peaty pools formed in the vast blanket bogs of the north-west, especially Caithness and Sutherland, hold 7 per cent of the total world resource of this unusual wetland. Loch Ness is a very fine example of a rare type of loch formed by a major geological fault. It also demonstrates the most significant physical characteristic of Scottish lochs – their depth – although at 276m/828ft it is easily surpassed by Loch Morar at 372m/1.116ft. Several of the lochs, gouged out by the great glaciers of the Ice Age, are amongst the deepest inland waters in the world.

Many of the rivers, especially in the Highlands, flow over hard quartzite rocks which are slightly acid and poor in nutrients; this makes both river and loch water unusually clear, even if the colour is peaty. The rivers of Scotland appear generally to differ depending on whether they flow east or west - the latter have small upland catchments on hard rocks, with marked changes in their flows in response to rain or snowfall, while eastern rivers drain larger catchments over softer rocks with only moderate fluctuations in flow. Western rivers are also low in nutrients and slightly acid throughout their whole length, and even a large eastward-flowing river such as the Dee in Aberdeenshire is of this character throughout most of its course.

Elsewhere, rivers such as the Tweed and the Don cross isolated bands of sandstone or carboniferous limestone in their lower reaches and are therefore much richer. Most rivers are fast flowing (about 20 per cent of river catchments in the Highland area have been modified by hydro-electric schemes) and there are only limited stretches where the typical slow-moving Lowland system can be seen – 'Ae link of the Forth is worth an earldom in the North' was the description of the fertile flat lands created by the meanders of this river near Stirling. Quite apart from their natural beauty, the river and loch systems of Scotland are renowned for their water quality and their fishing – Loch Lomond supports no fewer than 19 different species of fish, including arctic relicts such as the char and brown trout in localized populations which are genetically distinct. Of the 45 species of fish known in Britain, Scotland has 40, and that number is still increasing as fish, mainly from the south, colonise the northern waters, a number having been deliberately introduced for sport fishing.

Of all species, the salmon and trout are most closely associated with Scottish rivers and lochs, especially the great salmon rivers of the Spey, the Tay, the Tweed and the Dee. Scottish salmon was exported in huge quantities to Europe as far afield as Venice in the 14th century; a catch of 1,300 fish from a single pool of the Findhorn River in Morayshire was recorded in 1648. There are over 200 salmon rivers in Scotland and several place names include 'lax' (Laxford, Laxdale, etc.) which is the Norse word for salmon. On the Tay alone, 100,000 were caught in one season in the early 19th century and the same river is famous for fine freshwater pearls, now becoming increasingly scarce: Scotland has the greatest reserves of pearl mussel in Western Europe. The most recent reports are encouraging regarding the status of the otter in Scotland, that elusive and attractive animal, now found in rivers and lochs throughout most of the country with the exception of some areas in the south east. Some species of water plants such as the least yellow water lily and slender-leaved pondweed are largely confined to Scotland, which has many water species in common with North America, the sub-Arctic and Central Europe. Often these are at the extreme edges of their range, including both plants and insects such as caddis flies, water beetles and northern damselflies, several of which are extremely rare.

The lochs are especially important as safe roosts for wintering wildfowl: Scotland lies in the north-west European wintering area of many birds which breed within Arctic and sub-Arctic zones, including Iceland, Greenland, Canada, Scandinavia and northern Russia. Shallow nutrient-rich lochs such as Loch Leven are particularly valuable in this respect, with internationally important roosts of pink-footed and greylag geese, whooper swan and pochard, as well as wintering duck such as teal and tufted duck. The wintering range of the Greenland white-fronted goose lies entirely within Britain and approximately half of the population spends the winter in Scotland, at Loch Ken in Galloway, Loch Lomond and on Islay. Following recolonization by the osprey in the 1950s, Scotland now holds the entire British population of this spectacular fishing species, with over 50 pairs now breeding here. The fast-flowing rocky streams and rivers provide important habitats for the dipper, so conspicuous by its white chest and bobbing movement in rocky streams, and the grey wagtail with its characteristic long swooping flight along the banks of many rivers. The non-native mink, almost certainly an escapee from previous mink farms, has unfortunately colonised many areas, and causes considerable damage to other wildlife, especially young ducklings.

Loch Lomond, famed in song and story, is a very good example of a loch which, straddling the Highland Boundary Fault, demonstrates the characteristics of both the deep cold Highland loch and the shallower Lowland system; at the southern end, where the Endrick River forms a classic delta, it is less than 18m/6oft in depth, while the northern section reaches 180m/620ft - the third deepest water body in Britain. Since twice as much rain falls on the acid schist rocks of the northern catchment (320cm/116in per annum at Loch Sloy) as on the southern sandstones and carboniferous lavas, the loch is mainly low in nutrients – a typically clear, cold Highland loch. At 71sq km/28sq miles it is the largest loch in Britain and possibly the most important in Scotland in terms of wildlife conservation value. Lying across the highland-lowland divide, it has a wide range of plant and animal life; of the 2,000 flowering plant species growing in Britain, Loch Lomond and its immediate environs support about a quarter, largely as a result of its great geological diversity and long history of human activity. A new main road north along the west shore provides spectacular views for the motorist, but the quieter eastern road ending at Rowardennan offers more opportunities to walk and appreciate the natural beauties of this scenic area which has now been proposed as the first National Park in Scotland.

The story of the loch begins more than 50,000 years ago when a huge ice sheet passed very slowly by Ben Lomond, carving out a massive trench over 200m/656ft below sea level, and at the same time diverting into the Clyde a number of rivers that had previously flowed eastwards at its southern end by the sheer volume of deposited ice. With the melting of the ice about 10000 years ago, the district around Loch Lomond developed a thin covering of glacial soil supporting a few trees, and the whole area still shows many of the features of a late glacial landscape, also reflected in its wildlife. The loch is known for a very rare fish, the powan, a member of the salmon family, which like the char is a relict of the Ice Age, as is a black dwarf race of the river lamprey, also found among the 19 fish species of the loch and its inflowing rivers. New species are found from time to time, such as a freshwater mudworm new to science, which has subsequently been found in Loch Morar, although nowhere else in Britain. A number of other species take their name from the loch, such as the Loch Lomond dock, while the diversity of habitats on Loch Lomondside generally is reflected by the 21 native mammals (out of a total of 22 for Britain as a whole) which can be found on one local estate.

Loch Lomondside has abundant archaeological evidence of human activity from earliest times, some of the most interesting being the 'crannogs' or lake dwellings which provided a degree of security from attack. Many of the 38 islands were inhabited for defensive purposes, although this would probably have been of little help against the ravages of the Vikings who sailed up Loch Long, 'portaging' their longboats over Tarbet and sailing down Loch Lomond. There were a number of early Christian settlements, and from medieval times onwards the loch and its surroundings were actively exploited – timber for ship-building and charcoal smelting and oak bark for leather tanning - the material being taken to Glasgow by boat down the Clyde. Nowadays, with the largest concentration of Scotland's population on its doorstep, the industry of the loch is mainly tourism and recreation, providing an essential open-air lung for the many thousands of visitors who use it throughout the year. Not all of the activities are compatible; speed-boats and jetskiers compete with fishermen and yachting enthusiasts, while the density of walkers on the well-known route up Ben Lomond has inadvertently created a serious local erosion problem.

There are many parallels between Loch Lomond and the River Tay, selected here as an example of a Scottish river valley and estuary system. Like Lomondside, it too crosses the Highland Boundary Fault, displaying facets of both Highland and lowland Scotland. Whereas Loch Lomond is the largest loch, the Tay has the largest catchment area and the greatest water flow of any river in Britain, and gives its name to one of the most varied regions in the country. It rises in the far west of Scotland at over 994m/ 2,980ft on Ben Lui southwest of Tyndrum, running for nearly 193km/120miles to end in the North Sea east of Dundee. For 24km/15miles of its length, it forms a fine deep Highland loch, Loch Tay, surrounded by magnificent scenery including Ben Lawers at 1,333m/4,000ft. From here it flows on through very attractive wooded landscapes past Pitlochry to be joined by its major tributary, the Tummel, at Ballinluig and subsequently, below Perth, by the Earn, the last main tributary before the industrial city of Dundee. It is tidal as far as Perth, which smaller cargo boats can reach, although in its lower reaches the shifting sandbanks, on which seals can frequently be seen basking, can be a hazard at low tide. An unusual feature on the banks of the Carse of Gowrie near Errol are the extensive reed beds growing on the very rich fine silts deposited in this slow-moving stretch of the river, which have created the only reed-cutting industry in Scotland, used for thatching of roofs throughout the country. This is the haunt of large flocks of pinkfeet and greylag geese, always an evocative sight when their honking skeins are seen against a rose-streaked sky in a late autumn evening.

The Tay is one of the best known salmon rivers in Scotland, especially the middle section with its deep pools and extensive gravel beds, which produced the Scottish record of a fish weighing 29kg/64lb. It is estimated that 10,000 salmon are caught annually by anglers, with a further 50,000 taken by commercial netsmen near the mouth of the river. Public visitors can see large salmon passing up the fish ladder on Loch Faskally at Pitlochry, constructed to allow fish to bypass the large hydro-electric power station there. Although the pearl fishery has declined, there is still at least one regular professional pearl fisher. The estuary is renowned for its congregations of wintering wildfowl, especially for mixed flocks of pink-footed and greylag geese (the average number of all species of wildfowl is in excess of 17,000), but it is internationally important for holding up to 20,000 eider duck which feed on the large mussel beds near the mouth of the river. With its huge catchment and enormous water flows, combined with its tidal regime, the Tay is liable to very serious flooding which in recent years has caused substantial damage to both farmland and residential and industrial areas within the city of Perth, raising questions about integrated land use and river control planning along this important Scottish waterway.

Farmland

Shinbrae was a fine hill farm, well set upon the brae above its neighbours.
The farmhouse squared its shoulders to the four winds with a sullen dignity, and the steading stood out boldly behind its brazen austerity.

David Toulmin – *Hard Shining Corn* (1972)

There could hardly be a greater contrast than that between a tiny croft perched on a rocky Harris headland, facing the Atlantic rollers, and the great flowing fields of barley which are typical of the Berwickshire merse in the Tweed Valley, yet both are part of the enormously varied farming landscape of Scotland. Most of the land of Scotland is under some form of agricultural use, even if only as rough hill sheep ground. The relatively limited area of good low arable land is intensively farmed and fully utilised, and the recent history of this farmland is little different from elsewhere in Britain in the last 50 years. Before that, colourful plants such as poppy, cornflower, corncockle, bugloss and fumitory would have been common among our cereal crops, since these species favour the same rich soils and their seeds were extremely difficult to separate from cereal seeds. Now cleaner seeds, herbicides and modern agricultural techniques have all but banished them from the fields. This has certainly been the fate of the truly endemic Scots primrose, which until the agricultural improvements in Orkney was a relatively common species. Exceptions to this are the untreated meadows in some of the glen bottoms in Perthshire, for example, and the flag iris and bog myrtle marshes of the rougher field margins on the west coast and islands. In Wigtownshire, extensive low-level coastal moorlands with larger open water areas than those found on the east coast have not yet been reclaimed. This is in marked contrast to the peatland of the Forth Valley which was mostly removed two centuries ago to create the good agricultural land of the Carse of Stirling, now producing, with the addition of large quantities of fertiliser, ten tonnes of grass per hectare.

In recent years, the trend towards uniformity of cereal crops by use of chemicals has reduced the availability of suitable breeding and rearing areas for ground-nesting bird species, and the replacement of hay meadows by improved grassland cut early for silage has changed both the landscape and the opportunities for wildlife. Similarly the replacement of old farm buildings, full of nooks and crannies, by modern frame barns, has reduced the nesting habitat for typical farm species such as the barn owl. While ponds and wet areas were a feature of the old farmland, most of these have been drained or filled, so that the yellow globe flower and mauve wood cranesbill are no longer a feature of wet meadows. Many of these wetlands in the Lowlands are quite small; in the Borders, for example, over 50 per cent are less than half a hectare in extent. This makes them especially vulnerable to drainage and infilling to increase the cropping area. In the last 40 years wetlands in Tayside region have declined by 20 per cent, and the figure for other lowland districts will be similar.

The widening and straightening of ditches by machines now leaves little room for the development of the wetland vegetation favoured by many species of plants and insects. In addition, changes in agricultural practice such as the growing of winter crops have removed the old stubbles from the farming scene to the detriment of rooks and peewits for example, which used to feed in huge flocks on the insects of these open fields – the 92,000 pairs of peewits in Scotland represents 40 per cent of the total British breeding population. It is estimated that song thrushes on farmland declined by more than 70 per cent in only 5 years between 1969 and 1974. The corncrake has retreated to the most northwesterly areas where modern intensive agriculture has not yet taken a hold; it seems incredible that as late as the early 19th century Lord Cockburn could refer to the 'ceaseless rural corn-craikes nestling happily in the dewy grass' of what is now Queen Street Gardens in the New Town of Edinburgh! However in recent years considerable increased breeding success has been achieved through more sympathetic management regimes locally, and 45 calling males were recorded in Orkney in 1996 compared to only 6 in 1993. Changes in agriculture have helped to create conflicts between farmers and wildlife – while huge flocks of overwintering geese were tolerated on stubble fields or where potatoes had been harvested, they are far less welcome on grassland which has been specially improved by liming and fertilising, or on early winter cereals.

Today's rural landscape is a relatively modern one, formed of large fields laid out and enclosed during the Agricultural Revolution of the late 18th and early 19th centuries, in contrast to the much older feudal Anglo-Saxon landscape of southern England for example. From that time, large fields have been much more typical of Scotland than elsewhere in Britain, and except on a few estates in the south, there has not been the same tradition of management of ancient dense hedgerows. Many of the hedgerows of lowland Scotland have been removed in the last 40 years to accommodate mechanised agriculture: between 1946 and 1979 it is estimated that 6,640km/4,150miles of hedgerow were lost, including some 33 per cent of those in Lothian and Central Regions. Nowadays, the most natural lowland wildlife is often to be found in the remaining hedgerows and especially those roadside verges which have not been treated with modern chemicals. Here can still be found many of the plant and insect species previously common on cultivated land, and the Scottish Wildlife Trust has designated a number of these rich plant areas as reserves to be protected against early cutting or chemical treatment by road authorities. Even where the ground is not especially rich, grassland in these verges can support upwards of 150 different species of grasses and flowering herbs, including cocksfoot, Yorkshire fog, white clover and creeping thistle.

Among the richest wildlife habitats are the grounds and woodland policies of the larger estate houses, with their mixtures of tree and shrub species, often enhanced by artificial ponds and open parkland. An excellent example of this is the Hirsel, near Coldstream in the eastern Borders. Because it has been in the same ownership for over three and a half centuries (and before that was part of a Cistercian Priory from 1166) it has not been subject to the dramatic changes which have affected the surrounding agricultural landscape - nearly a fifth of its 1,200ha/3,000 acres are still woodland of many different deciduous and conifer species: elsewhere in the district, native broadleaf woodland has largely been converted to farmland or replaced by pure conifer plantations. The Hirsel Lake (created in 1787) is an important wildlife reservoir for this whole area, as the largest stretch of open water within a 20 mile radius, supporting up to 2,000 mallard ducks, in addition to large populations of shoveler, tufted duck and goldeneye – the estate as a whole has 100 breeding bird species with a further 60 regularly seen, reflecting its great range of habitats. Such estates have often retained a diversity of those marginal semi-natural situations – open water, marshland, reedbed, woodland and scrub which the modern farm has eliminated in its drive to increase crop yields.

The main distinction between Scotland and the rest of Britain is the proportion of upland and low ground, and often the conjunction between Highlands and Lowlands provides some of the most valuable wildlife habitat. Lapwings and oyster catchers frequently resort to grazed upland fields during the breeding season, while in bad weather in spring flocks of golden plover, normally found on the upper moorland, can often be seen on the richer ground around farmsteads. Curlew and twite favour old croft land which has been manured by domestic stock over a long period and sheep carrion has been an important element in the survival of predatory birds in the hills. The boundary of fields, at least in the glens, have traditionally been dry stane dykes i.e. unmortared walls, which are such a conspicuous feature of the Scottish countryside. In such exposed landscapes, these provide important shelter for a surprising range of wildlife, but are too often nowadays replaced by fencing which does not provide the same habitat. Farms and their immediately surrounding land in the uplands generally create small oases for wildlife, especially where there are protective shelter belts and kitchen gardens: the concentration of domestic stock often enhances insect life and attracts more bird species than would otherwise be found on the open hill.

CHAPTER 5

A People with a Past

*For that is the mark of the Scot of all classes: that he stands
in an attitude towards the past unthinkable to Englishmen
..... and there burns alive in him a sense of identity with the
dead even to the twentieth generation.*

Robert Louis Stevenson – *Weir of Hermiston* 1894

WE KNOW FROM THE oldest archaeological evidence found on the
island of Rum, that there was human habitation in Scotland
between 8-9,000 years ago, not long after much of the land had
become habitable following the retreat of the great ice glaciers. It
is quite possible that man had reached Scotland as far back as
14,000 years ago. These hunter-gatherers would have followed the
seaboard, pushing further north according to the season in search
of food: wanderers who survived on what they could collect, trap
or hunt with primitive weapons. We know also from the vast mid-
dens around estuaries such as the Tay, that they consumed great
quantities of shell-fish, and flint remains indicate that they were
able to catch fish and fur bearing animals such as beaver and bear.
It is estimated that the permanent population towards the end of
this Mesolithic period was around 10,000.

The first truly settled populations came with the Stone Age
around 4000 BC, with the arrival of tribes from Western Europe
and England skilled in raising domestic animals and cultivating
crops. It is clear from the range of cereals grown in northern latitudes and at relatively high altitudes that the climate was more
favourable than at present. Even with primitive stone axes, they
must have been capable of clearing quite substantial areas of
woodland, which could then be kept open by a combination of
fire and grazing animals.

These farmers penetrated as far as the Northern Isles, where
there are some of the finest surviving examples of their way of life
in, for example, the Stone Age village of Skara Brae or the awe-
inspiring burial chambers of Maeshowe, both in Orkney. They

erected the ceremonial stone circles which can be found at Stenness in Orkney and the famed standing stones of Callanish on Lewis. They constructed permanent houses of stone and timber, fashioned pottery and jewellery of stone and bone, and imported flints. They had the means of travel along waterways and by sea.

With the use of metal in the Bronze and Iron Ages, settlers in Scotland had the capacity to make their mark on the environment, and from the evidence available, made substantial inroads into the forest, not least for the cutting of timber to make charcoal for iron smelting. Spades and simple ploughs were fashioned, while gold was used for finer articles and embellishment. Much of our knowledge of these people is derived from their distinctive burial systems, including beaker graves and cremation. Towards the end of this period, the accumulation of peat indicated a deterioration in the climate which became wetter and cooler, with resultant movements in population. Iron-age hilltop forts are common throughout Scotland, often with quite elaborate defensive ramparts of vitrified stone enclosing small settlements of wooden houses. This period also saw the construction of massive tower-like stone fortifications known as brochs, usually situated on good defensive situations along the northern coasts, which are quite unique in Europe.

Around the first century AD there is the first appearance of people who can be identified as Celts, having moved northwards from central and northern Europe. Apart from their aptitude for making war, they brought with them their distinctive Brythonic language and considerable skills as horsebreeders, farmers, and craftsmen in metalwork, pottery, and wood. The Picts, or "painted ones" largely inhabiting northern and eastern Scotland beyond the Forth, were a Celtic people apparently resulting from the merging of local tribes about the 4th century AD, especially noted for their fine stone carvings and military organisation which subsequently proved troublesome to the invading Romans. Indeed, the Roman occupation of southern Scotland lasted little over 100 years and their impact appears to have been relatively modest. Other Brythonic-speaking tribal groupings formed kingships centred on Edinburgh, Dumbarton and the Solway. However the Picts as a discrete group disappeared around the 9th century, apparently absorbed by the Scots from northern Ireland who established their kingdom initially in Argyll in the 5th and 6th centuries and subsequently spread northwards and eastwards to supplant the Britons of Strathclyde, and eventually in the 10th century, overcoming the Angles of Lothian.

With the coming of St. Ninian to Whithorn on the Solway in the 5th century and preceding St. Columba's arrival in Scotland in the following century, the Christian Church became a powerful influence, almost extinguished by the ravages of the Viking invasions from the latter half of the 8th century onwards, although in due course the Norsemen too were converted to Christianity. Based on the Northern Isles, these sea-borne raiders pillaged the western coasts and islands, overcoming the Picts and Scots in the northlands from the early 9th century. They also formed settled communities in the north and west, became accomplished farmers and traders between bouts of seasonal raiding, and left a profound mark on the culture of the Northern Isles in particular, including a legacy of language which is particularly evident in place names and in local land tenure.

The last major "invasion" was by the Anglo-Normans and Flemings mainly in the 12th century, invited by David I to act as stewards and administrators of different segments of his kingdom. They started a system of feudalism which in a number of ways has persisted to the present time. Together with the major monastic houses, their castles dotted throughout the south and east of Scotland would have had a very considerable impact on the surrounding land. The castle was a township in miniature and indeed the characteristic burghs of Scotland often formed around such focal points. The occupants of the castles drew upon the natural resources of the local countryside for its means of sustenance, in the form of timber, fuel, building materials, food, and grazing lands, and through the feudal system, used the human resources for men-at-arms and labour. For some time beforehand, there was a gradual movement from the hills of the previously mainly pastoral people down into the cleared valleys, increasing the area of arable cultivation, especially in the more fertile eastern lowlands, and with a progressive enlargement of sheep flocks at the expense of cattle.

Usually situated on the most fertile lands, the great church houses were particularly important in introducing new crops and forms of agriculture from the continent, and were pre-eminent in developing the wool trade, encouraging the opening up of grazing lands. It is estimated that the combined sheep flocks of the eight Cistercian monasteries numbered over 40,000 animals. Huge amounts of building materials and other resources would have been required for the construction and maintenance of the abbeys, which were the largest and most important centres of their kind for many miles around, and were so crucial to the development of many of the first towns. The establishment of such impressive monuments alongside the building of royal castles and the laying out of burghs (with enough surpluses of food and other commodities to support cash markets) indicate that Scotland during this early medieval period was not, by the standards of the time, a poor country. This is confirmed by the increase in population between the 11th and 13th centuries, estimated at a million people by the end of this period.

Between the 12th and 16th centuries, sheep and cattle formed the basis of trade with the Low Countries, France and the Baltic, the main products being wool, hides, and skins. Increasingly, as skills developed these were converted into manufactured goods such as leather and cloth. There was also an increasing export of fish and salt. However, this progress of trade and industry was considerably affected by the 13th and 14th century Wars of Independence and not least by the Black Death, which took a huge toll on the population. By the 11th century most readily habitable land was already settled, and it was not until the 16th century population expansion that there was pressure on the much more marginal land, and a fresh surge of clearance of 'waste', or rough uncultivated ground. Since early times, the land itself had been farmed on a system of infields and outfields, grouped around a fermtoun of primitive agricultural dwellings, where the major tenants or husbandmen would be supported by up to two dozen cottars on much smaller holdings. The husbandmen were usually limited to one year leases, with the rents dependent on the previous year's harvest and were required during feudal times to serve in the lord's army when the need arose.

There is good evidence that the Norman and Flemish incomers fused their feudal systems with the native culture, which was dominated by Irish elements. Through intermarriage with the Celtic aristocracy and by adaptation of custom and language, a hybrid kingdom was created by the 12th century, with the Celts themselves adopting their own brand of feudalism. The second wave of Flemings established themselves north of the Forth, but by the 14th century, these colonists had become naturalised to the extent of forming a distinctive Highland culture, largely based on the Gaelic language which separated them linguistically and in other ways from the increasingly Scots-speaking lowlanders. Out of this there developed a very loose and fluid clann (meaning simply 'children', embracing a number of families when expedient) grouping, the term "clan system" being a simplistic mid-19th century invention.

The basic cultural difference between Highland and Lowland society (apart from language) was the emphasis on the importance of kinship, albeit modified by feudalism, north and west of the Forth, which survived right up to the Risings of the 18th century. So-called clan chiefs did not need to hold land as such and few clans had the distinct territories ascribed to them by later promoters of 'tartanry', nor were the clansfolk all blood-related – Highland society was by no means exclusively Celtic. Land was regarded as a heritable trusteeship rather than as a resource to be exploited for its cash returns. Nor was their reputation for lawlessness entirely justified: the McDonalds who held the Lordship of the Isles were noted for their peaceful and civilised lifestyle in the 14th and 15th centuries, while the most notorious outlaw, the 'Wolf of Badenoch' who ravaged the north east of Scotland, was descended from the Norman Stewarts. Nevertheless, the Highlanders were stereotyped as wild feckless barbarians for centuries until their equally mythological and romantic reincarnation by the Victorians.

Life in Scotland until the mid-18th century was dominated by natural environmental circumstances and people were still very much at the mercy of the elements – a poor growing season could result in very serious famine, as happened in the last decade of the 17th century, while the narrow range of crops grown was determined by the limited area and quality of arable land. Villages on the English model, with a few exceptions, were unknown, being replaced by more scattered agricultural settlements. Oats provided the 'staff of life' – until the later introduction of the potato – and were eaten in a variety of forms. Like other cereals, they were often imported from the Lowlands, while the main export from the Highlands was cattle and other livestock. Cattle in fact increased in value by a factor of three in the latter half of the 18th century, while oats doubled in value. However, descriptions of the houses of the peasantry in the Highlands in the previous century indicate that these were little better than the most primitive mud huts, providing living conditions comparable to the most backward of developing countries to-day.

A major change occurred with the onset of the agricultural revolution in the Lowlands from 1760 onwards, with for example, the introduction of the turnip which allowed stock, previously killed and salted, to be kept over winter for the first time. The development of new drainage techniques, liming, enclosure, and crop rotation led to progressive land improvement, while the introduction of new breeds of domestic animals and crops provided higher yields. New ploughs and machinery enabled a much greater area to be brought under cultivation, spurred by the demand of the growing industrial cities. By the end of the 18th century, the old clan had largely disappeared, as the traditional relationship between the chief and his followers broke down, and a cash economy substituted for barter and subsistence. With the demand for Highland produce, including the lucrative kelp used in industrial processes, many Highland landowners became relatively wealthy and increasingly adopted expensive southern lifestyles. This in turn, coupled with the marked rise in the price of wool at this time, prompted landowners to raise rents and encourage the establishment of large sheep flocks at the expense of the resident crofters, who were increasingly forced on to poorer land on the coast in the notorious Clearances.

Undoubtedly, the worsening conditions were partly fuelled by rapid increases in local populations. The overall population in the Highlands rose from 115,000 in 1751 to over 200,000 by 1831. The situation was made worse by the traditional sub-division of land and by the periodic 19th century famines. The impact of the Clearances was particularly felt in certain localities – some 700 families were removed from the Sutherland Estates between 1807 and 1821, although this was exceptional. Four out of ten families were evicted from Ardnamurchan over the 10 year period from 1846, mainly at the hands of commercially-minded trustees who had frequently taken over bankrupt estates. Another source of revenue for landowners was military recruitment for the British Army, relying at least in part on the ancestral loyalty of the Highlanders, to raise local regiments which it is estimated numbered between some 40,000 and 75,000 men between 1756 and 1815. No doubt this ready recruitment was assisted by worsening domestic conditions, especially after 1846 when the potato famine struck and when by the end of that year, three-quarters of the population had no food left. A huge tragedy was largely averted, not so much by government intervention, but by charitable organisations who frequently provided relief in return for labour. What became known as the 'Destitution Roads' in the North West, for example, were built by crofters who were unable to survive on their meagre produce.

It was hardly surprising that the drift to the expanding industrial cities accelerated: by 1836 there were 22,000 Highlanders in Glasgow, and by the 1890's no less than three out of ten of Greenock's population had been born in the Highlands. Meanwhile, that great religious schism of 1843 known as the Disruption, when 470 ministers of the Church of Scotland seceded to form the Free Church (mainly in the Highlands and Islands) effectively ended the monopoly of power by the established church and the demise of "the parish state". The generous support given to the break-away church is reflected in the 44,000 children who were being taught in Free Church Schools a mere 4 years later. This same church, in contrast to the Church of Scotland, played a significant part in highlighting the plight of the dispossessed crofters and bringing this to the attention of the official

Napier Commission. The resulting Crofters Holdings Act of 1884 went some way towards remedying the injustices inflicted on them.

The latter half of the 19th century saw the last major migrations into Scotland from Ireland, mainly from the south, who for the first time since before the Reformation, established significant Catholic elements in the population. However, in the 1870's Irish Protestants from Ulster, under the influence of worsening agricultural conditions there, outnumbered all other Irish immigrants. Both of these waves contributed to the religious and cultural sectarianism which has left its mark up to the present day especially in west central Scotland. There have been relatively few other immigrants, mostly from the Indian sub-continent in recent decades. From the 1960s onwards there has been a small but steadily increasing number of people from England taking up residence in Scotland, either as professionals working in the capital or retiring to the more attractive rural towns.

Scotland's history is carried forward in today's culture and institutions. Those which are considered distinctive, in a UK context, are the law, religion and education, all of which have affinities with European systems, reflecting the close connections which Scotland has had in the past, notably with France, Germany, Switzerland, the Low Countries and the Baltic. This fruitful interchange included military and political alliances, trade, religious philosophy, and university education, all of which tended to give Scots a Continental outlook which may in part explain their relatively pro-European sympathies. Certainly those in Western Europe would appreciate Scottish Law, with its emphasis on principle and 'common sense' rather than precedent, while the democratic church governance of the Church of Scotland, with its separation from the Crown and insistence on theological scholarship, would appeal to Protestant European countries. In the field of education, Scotland has still retained the ideal of a broad curriculum accessible to all, despite the relatively recent movement towards informal school grading.

That history is also evident in a distinctive culture and in the arts. There is a new confidence in our past which has successfully melded the new with the old, as in, for example, popular Gaelic rock music and the resurgence of dance and a modern form of ceilidh (a social gathering, often with dance) which appeals to young people - the same young people who after dancing a Saturday night away, possibly on behalf of some environmental charity, may be found walking the hills on the following day. Musical instruments such as the ancient clarsach or small harp are being taught to increasing numbers of youngsters, while the traditional pipes can be heard playing in ways no pipe major of the past would have dreamt of. There is a flourishing folk music scene, going beyond the kitsch, and unashamedly telling the story of the times. There has been a real renaissance in Scottish literature over the last 20 years, using a new language and idiom, and likewise in drama, often reflecting popular folk experience. Not only Gaelic, but Scots is also undergoing something of a revival – it was not anticipated that William Lorimer's New Testament in authentic Scots published 15 years ago would become a best-seller. All of this is evidence of a vibrant and robust culture, not ossified by its history, but not forgetting it either. In the rather partial view of Paul H Scott, introducing Scotland: A Concise Cultural History:

"In all the arts, this Scottishness is now more vigorous and self-confident than at any time since Westminster began to interfere in Scottish affairs after Waterloo".

For I am half a Scot by birth and bred a whole one..........

Lord Byron – *Don Juan* 1819-24

CHAPTER 6

A Diversity of Regions

I could not find any Scottish way of life that would embrace all the ways of life that I had observed from the time I left Edinburgh for the Borders, the Borders for Glasgow, and Glasgow for the Highlands.

Edwin Muir – *Scottish Journey* (1935)

TO HIGHLIGHT THE DIVERSITY of Scotland's regions five broad geographical regions have been identified below and the main population centres within each are briefly described. The conventional division between highland and lowland Scotland has been avoided, since the lowlands on the coast extend as far north as Caithness, while Highland country comes almost to the boundaries of Glasgow in the south.

Galloway and the Borders

This queer compromise between fairyland and battle-ground which is the Border.

H V Morton – *In Search of Scotland* (1929)

The southern reaches of Scotland encompass a great variety of countryside, from the rugged hill country of the Merrick in Western Galloway to the rich lowland farms of the lower Tweed Valley in the east. The economy is based on agriculture and forestry, with relatively little manufacturing industry beyond the declining traditional textiles in the Border towns and few large population centres. The climate in the west favours stock rearing, while the east has some of the best dry arable land in the country. There are also considerable climatic differences between the mild, sheltered Solway coast and the extremes of the massif of the cen

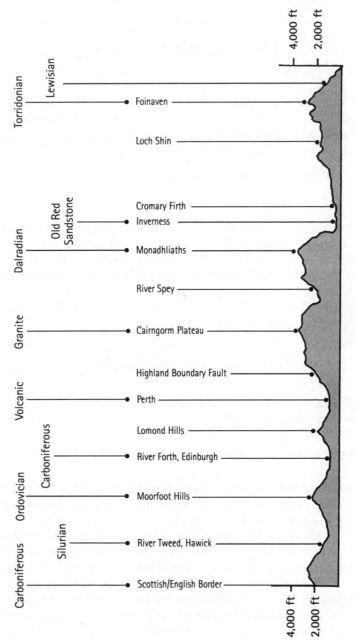

Transect of mainland Scotland from south-east to north-west

4,000 ft
2,000 ft

Torridonian

Lewisian

Foinaven

Loch Shin

Old Red Sandstone

Dalradian

Cromary Firth
Inverness
Monadhliaths

River Spey

Granite

Cairngorm Plateau

Volcanic

Highland Boundary Fault

Perth

Carboniferous

Lomond Hills

River Forth, Edinburgh

Ordovician

Moorfoot Hills

Silurian

River Tweed, Hawick

Carboniferous

Scottish/English Border

4,000 ft
2,000 ft

tral uplands, where the mean daily minimum temperature in January is frequently below freezing. Some of the highest annual rainfall levels in Scotland have been recorded at Loch Dee in West Galloway, whereas the coastal areas of Berwickshire have some of the longest periods of sunshine each year. The tropical plants grown outdoors in the Logan Gardens (in the Rhinns of Galloway) testify to the mildness of this local climate which, under the influence of the Gulf Stream, provides some of the highest winter temperatures in Scotland.

The whole region lies to the south of the Southern Upland Fault, bounded to the south by both the Solway Firth and the steeply rising Cheviot Hills which straddle the border. The River Tweed rises in the central hills (not far from the source of the Clyde) and the rich arable farmland of its basin is fringed to the north by the low plateaus of the Moorfoot and Lammermuir Hills, forming a horseshoe round this great valley. To the west, the rounded Southern Uplands are broken by the rugged higher granite masses of Criffel, Cairnsmore and the highest hill in the region, the Merrick, at 921m/2,765ft. The few north-south routes through this range follow the river valleys flowing into the Solway Firth: the Esk, Annan, Nith and Dee.

Despite the extent of upland forestry, the region is characterised by great sweeps of open grassy hills and heather moorland, and supports a rich wildlife. Wild goats are found in the Moffat Hills and the Glen Trool area in the west, while the coasts are especially notable for wintering wildfowl from the arctic region, taking advantage of the saltmarshes and vast mudflats of the Solway shore, and the seabird colonies of the east coast cliffs. In western Galloway, the moist climate has favoured the development of deep peat bogs known as 'flowes'. Although native deciduous forests have been greatly reduced, there are old coppice oak and mixed woodlands in several of the river valleys, especially the Dee and the Cree, leading to the Solway Firth – in spring, these are covered with sheets of colourful bluebells.

Overall the population density is low and the culture is rural; industry is still tied to natural resources, including woollens derived from local sheep and food processing dependent on the dairy produce of the western pastures. There are still important local fishing communities such as Eyemouth on the east coast, and throughout the area commercial forestry plantations have expanded considerably in the last 40 years. Although there are no large resorts, the rolling, unspoiled countryside and rich historic interest attract an increasing number of discriminating tourists, now an important element in the economy of the region. Place names reflect the mixture of peoples who have settled the area, from the ancient British and Celtic tribes in the west to the Angles and Saxons in the east, with much influence from Vikings and later, Norman aristocrats. The latter had difficulty in subduing the turbulent Celtic chiefs and Galloway was one of the last places in southern Scotland to lose the Gaelic tongue.

Dumfries (pop 32,000), on the banks of the River Nith seven miles from the Solway, is still an important agricultural market town, reflecting the main industry of the region and its historical association with the Irish cattle trade. At one time it was the major port for south-west Scotland, occupying a strategic position at a convenient crossing-point of the Nith on one of the main routes to Carlisle in the south. The town is now by-passed by the much improved A75 connecting to the ferry terminal at Stranraer. Although it is the oldest and most important burgh in the western Borders, it was far enough away to escape the ravages of Border warfare which afflicted towns such as Berwick over centuries. Manufacturing industries include food processing based primarily on dairy produce and high-quality knitwear and hosiery. The lower Nith supports a unique haaf-net salmon fishery, the name reflecting its ancient Norse origin.

West Central

Loch Lomond lies quite near to Glasgow. Nice Glaswegians motor out there and admire the scenery and calculate its horse-power and drink whisky and chaff one another in genteelly Anglicised Glaswegianisms.

Lewis Grassic Gibbon (with Hugh MacDiarmid) – *Scottish Scene* (1934)

Lying across the Highland Boundary Fault, which defines the northern edge of the central lowland plain, these administrative areas incorporate Lowlands and Highlands. The new local authority districts include both large rural areas such as Argyll and South Lanarkshire as well as the several predominantly urban districts such as East Renfrew in the Greater Glasgow conurbation. Stirling area is the true heartland of Scotland, with its centre in the historic town of Stirling itself, but Glasgow is undoubtedly the commercial hub. The area is dominated by the Clyde Valley; the river rises high in the Southern Uplands and its banks support much of the heavy industry which made it famous in the latter part of the 19th century. Immediately to the south of the Highland Boundary Fault lie a number of low volcanic hill areas such as the Campsie Fells, Kilpatrick Hills and the Ochils, forming a crescent of foothills which give way in the north to the much grander range of Breadalbane, and in the west to Ben Lomond, Ben Vorlich and the mountains of Argyll.

On either side of the River Forth, there are a number of old crossing routes from Highlands to Lowlands, via the River Teith at Callander and Strathallan at Stirling. Glasgow itself lies in a basin formed by the foothills to the north and the Renfrew Heights to the south-west, its outskirts a mere 32km/20miles from the southern end of the famed Loch Lomond, largest of the Scottish lochs. Apart from its freshwater lochs, this ancient kingdom of Strathclyde has some impressive sea lochs with outlets into the Clyde Estuary such as Loch Long, the Gareloch and Loch Striven. To the south of Glasgow, the Clyde coast forms a low-lying strip widening to the south and developing inland into the broad moorlands of Ayrshire. As Glasgow's population grew, the Ayrshire dairy industry became increasingly important to supply its needs. Off the Ayrshire coast, sheltered from the Atlantic by the long finger of the Kintyre peninsula in South Argyll, the island of Arran represents a microcosm of lowland and highland Scotland, with the Highland Boundary Fault running through its centre.

This huge area also takes in the mountainous inner Hebridean islands of Mull and Jura and lower-lying Islay and Tiree on its north-western border, which could hardly offer a greater contrast to its industrial centres. Because of this diversity, it is almost impossible to define the character of the region: from the highly developed and populous basin of the Clyde, the cradle of Scottish heavy industry, to the remoteness of the Paps of Jura, where deer easily outnumber humans, and which have more in common with the Highlands proper than central Scotland. The region's climate is mild and damp, although low-lying Tiree claims the sunshine record for Britain, and the resort towns of the Clyde coast have the lowest rainfall in the west of Scotland. The variation in rainfall is demonstrated by the fact that Stirling receives less than half that of Loch Lomond only 32km/20miles to the west.

The coalfields of Lanarkshire and Ayrshire were the basis of the heavy iron and steel industries which grew up along the Clyde Valley and which provided the materials for ship-building and locomotive manufacture. These have now been superseded by a range of high technology industries and services. Agriculture is still important, especially in the fertile middle Clyde Valley and the Ayrshire hinterland, while tourism, traditionally associated with areas such as Loch Lomond, the Trossachs, and the Clyde Coast, is one of the fastest-growing sectors of the economy. Argyll's fish farming has increased rapidly in recent years, based on its numerous sea lochs.

Glasgow (pop 623,850) is the largest city in Scotland and in the heyday of Empire was second only to London in commercial importance. Although economic development came relatively late to Glasgow, its position on the Clyde with ready access to the west favoured trade with the American colonies in the 18th century. Glasgow merchants made their fortunes in tobacco, sugar and cotton, and subsequently invested in the growing industries founded on nearby coal and iron ores, which earned for the city and its hinterland the title 'Workshop of the Empire', pre-eminent in ship building. The Clyde was deepened, linking canals were constructed, and Port Glasgow became a hive of maritime activity. Banking and textiles also became important and the booming growth following the Industrial Revolution drew in large numbers of workers from Ireland and the Highlands. The demise of heavy industries hit the Clyde Valley especially hard during the Depression of the early 1930s, but massive post-war slum clearance, the translation of traditional skills into light engineering and high-tech industries, and the development of the service sector, notably finance, have created a 'post-industrial' city with an invigorating cultural life which has attracted international attention.

Fife and the Lothians

I wish you were in Edinboro' with me - it is quite lovely - bits of it.

Oscar Wilde, - *letter to E W Godwin,* 17 December 1884

The Kingdom of Fife, as proud Fifers like to call it, sits comfortably between the great rivers of Tay and Forth, a peninsula of gently undulating farmland in the east, with scattered mining settlements in the west. Only one of the deep coal mines is now in operation, and many of the previously scarred landscapes have been reclaimed for agriculture or recreation. Separated from the rest of the country by the Ochil Hills to the west, Fife is bounded on the east by the North Sea, with attractive old coastal fishing villages and ports long associated with Continental Europe. This coast and its whitewashed villages attract many visitors, drawn also by the medieval town of St Andrews. There is fertile farmland in the Howe of Fife in the north-east of the region and, although very little of the original deciduous forest remains, at Tentsmuir on the mouth of the Tay is one of the largest sand dune systems in the country, now extensively afforested with pine.

Across the Forth in the Lothians, the coastal plain is noted for its high-quality agricultural crops, based on a dry climate and rich red sandstone soils. As in Fife, there is evidence of recent coal mining, and of oil shale in the heaps of rust-coloured waste in West Lothian. To the south of Edinburgh the heathery Pentland Hills (highest point 607m/1840ft) stretch almost to the upper Clyde Valley. Isolated volcanic masses and plugs punctuate the landscape, for example North Berwick Law, and the spectacular 100m/300ft Bass Rock in the Firth of Forth, with its internationally renowned gannetry.

Raised beaches are a feature of both the Lothian and Fife coasts, on which many of the area's fine golf courses, such as St Andrews and Gullane, are situated. The southern and eastern boundaries of the region are formed by the Moorfoot Hills and the Lammermuirs on the northern edge of the Southern Uplands, used for both hill sheep-farming and game-shooting. These are crossed by ancient routes once used by invaders from the south, and by drovers taking cattle down from the Highlands to the southern markets. This long-settled landscape, where cultivation was relatively easy, boasts many of the finest mansions and estates of Scotland. The River Forth, the only river of any consequence in this region, was renowned as a fishery in medieval times, noted especially for its oysters and mussels. Now it is a busy commercial waterway, with a constant traffic of container ships and oil tankers bound for the oil terminal at Hound Point near Edinburgh and the great petrochemical complex of Grangemouth upriver.

Coal, which was used as far back as the Middle Ages to evaporate coastal salt, was the basis of the Industrial Revolution in this area, but has now become insignificant. Inshore fishing is still carried out, but intensive farming, with much of the produce being utilised locally by centres of population such as Edinburgh, is still very important. The early establishment of universities and colleges created a demand for paper and a very substantial brewing industry developed, centred on good water supplies around Edinburgh. The economy of the region is diverse, including defence equipment, electronics and computing, and a wide range of services to support the many commercial and financial institutions of the capital and its satellites.

This is one of the drier regions of Scotland, and the annual rainfall in Edinburgh, distributed evenly throughout the year, is similar to that of Rome. However, it is also known for the chilling sea mist or haar from the North Sea which is a feature of summer months. Temperatures vary considerably with proximity to the sea, but snow is relatively rare and does not lie for long on low ground. Cool east winds are common, and, combined with the prevailing westerlies channelled by the Forth-Clyde gap, make this a turbulent area, particularly along the coast.

Edinburgh (pop 441,620) is reputed to be the capital of the ancient British kingdom of Goddodin ruled by King Myndogg, and there is certainly evidence of an Iron Age fort where the castle now stands, confirming its defensive importance. Until the Union of the Parliaments in 1707, the city was the location of the Scottish Parliament, and therefore the government capital of the country. The seven volcanic hills of the city all offer dramatic prospects across the Forth and over the Pentlands to the south. The port of Leith has provided ready access to Europe (especially the Baltic) over a considerable period, and much of Edinburgh's prosperity in the Middle Ages was built on wool exported through this port. The so-called New Town, begun in the middle of the 18th century, is an outstanding example of disciplined Georgian town planning and architecture on a grand scale, contrasting with the comfortable disorder of the Old Town between the castle and the Royal Palace of Holyrood. Given its wealth of history and attractive architecture it is not surprising that tourism is a main-stay of the city's economy, but Edinburgh is also the adminstrative centre of Scotland (at the time of writing anticipating a devolved Parliament), with a very high percentage of employees in the public sector. Apart from the traditional industries mentioned above, Edinburgh has developed as an important financial centre, with a concentration of investment houses, banks, and pension and insur-ance companies to rival London. With three universities and sever-al colleges, it provides for education and research over a wide vari-ety of disciplines. The capital is also the centre for a number of legal and medical institutions, is renowned for its annual International Arts Festival, and has a high proportion of Scotland's museums and art galleries.

Grampian and Tayside

This is the East coast with winter
Written into its constitution,
And so is very productive of men
Who do not wait for good
In case there is none.

George Bruce – *Praising Aberdeenshire Farmers*

These are the regions of the great salmon rivers – the Tay, Spey, Dee and Don – all rising in the central Highlands, which curve in a great arc along their western boundaries. The older regional names referred to above now include the new council areas of Angus, Perthshire and Kinross and Aberdeenshire. Here is found every landscape formation from high mountain plateau to dra-matic cliff coastline and river estuary, interspersed with some of the richest farmland in the country along the Carse of Gowrie and Strathmore. The hard-working Protestant culture of the farming communities celebrated by George Bruce above also reflects the harsher environment of the exposed Mearns of Kincardine (where my boyhood remembrance of planting potatoes in the bitter winds of March from the North Sea confirms Bruce's comment) and the great plain of Buchan north of Aberdeen, much of it reclaimed from peat bog and rock by industrious farmers in the 18th and 19th centuries. This was the land of the Picts, with their southern kingdom based in central Angus, who left behind only their finely carved stones dotted throughout the Lowlands.

The river systems determine much of the topography and patterns of settlement. The Spey, probably the most turbulent main river in Britain, is the only one flowing northwards into the Moray Firth; the others end their courses in the North Sea. With the largest catchment of any river in the country, the Tay flows from the highly scenic Breadalbane Mountains and Loch Tay in north Perthshire, through the alluvial deposits of the rich Carse of Gowrie to form a wide estuary at Dundee. Both the Dee and the Don have their sources high in the eastern Cairngorms, cutting through hard granites in their upper reaches and eventually bracketing the city of Aberdeen at the coast.

Apart from the Cairngorm massif, with several peaks above 1,333m/4,000ft, and the mountain systems of north and west Perthshire, there are lower volcanic outcrops in the Sidlaw and Ochil Hills. These lie to the south of the Highland Boundary Fault which cuts through this region from Stonehaven south-westwards. Like the spokes of a wheel, the many tributaries of the main river systems radiate outwards from the central plateau of the Grampians to create attractive glens such as Glen Isla, Glen Clova and Glen Avon, in earlier times the only routes through this mountain barrier. The large lochs of Tayside, from Loch Rannoch in the north to Loch Earn in the south, are enticing landscape features and attract many tourists to the area. The coastline ranges from the huge sand dune systems north of Aberdeen to the spectacular sea cliffs south of Peterhead and Stonehaven.

Although the climate of the eastern Lowlands of the region is dry, with high sunshine records along the coast, at the western end of Loch Tay the annual rainfall averages 1,524mm/60in. Areas such as Strathmore and Moray are sheltered from the wetter weather by the protecting Cairngorms. Altitude is especially important here in determining temperature: Braemar, at 339m/1,017ft and well inland, has recorded a winter temperature of -27.2°C: at lower levels, inland towns such as Crieff in Perthshire have relatively high summer temperatures. In common with other eastern areas, sea mist is a feature of the coast.

There are marked contrasts in the economy of the area between the industrial centres of Dundee and Aberdeen and the rural hinterland. Game sports, deer stalking and grouse shooting occupy extensive areas in the Angus glens and Upper Donside, combined with forestry and upland farming, while the lowlands are noted for soft fruits grown in Tayside, cereal in the drier lowlands, and beef cattle in Aberdeenshire. The rivers of Speyside and the grain-growing areas of Morayshire combine to make this a centre for whisky distilling. The traditional textile industries of Dundee and its satellite towns in Angus have been largely replaced by electronics and light manufacturing, although shipbuilding and repairing have been given a boost by North Sea oil development. Queen Victoria's patronage of Deeside helped the early establishment of a thriving tourist industry, and the two ski centres in the area have brought valuable employment during the winter months.

The two main centres of Aberdeen (pop 218,220) and Dundee (pop 153,710) are both important local ports with long-standing connections with the Baltic, a history of shipbuilding, and associations with the development of the whaling industry in the 18th and 19th centuries: Dundee was at one time the chief whaling port in Britain (whale oil was used for softening jute). Both have now benefited from North Sea oil developments, although this has transformed the economy of Aberdeen to a far greater extent than that of Dundee. Aberdeen has always been an important market for its large agricultural hinterland and one of the premier fishing ports in Britain – it is still the main port in Scotland for white fish. By contrast, the textile industry, especially the introduction of jute, pushed the population of Dundee from 26,000 to 160,000 over the course of the 19th century, a very high proportion of the working population being women employed in these industries. Much of the old town of Dundee has been demolished and there is considerable new commercial and leisure development of its waterside. As the offshore oil capital of Europe, Aberdeen now has the busiest helicopter port in the world, and has seen its harbour adapt from the herring boom of 100 years ago to the repair and servicing technology demanded by the oil bonanza off its shores.

Highlands and Islands

*Lord Aberdeen was quite touched when I told him I was
so attached to the dear,
dear Highlands and missed the fine hills so much. There is
a great peculiarity
about the Highlands and Highlanders.*

Queen Victoria, – *quoted in Victoria in the Highlands ed. D
Duff* (1968)

If we substitute 'distinctiveness' for 'peculiarity', it is easier to
appreciate Queen Victoria's comment, for this is a unique region,
which for many epitomises Scotland. Lying entirely to the north of
the Highland Boundary Fault, this is an area dominated by its
mountain landscapes, deep glens, lochs and literally hundreds of
islands. The Highlands and Islands now represent one of the most
extensive semi-natural areas in Europe, attracting many thousands
of visitors each year to experience its rugged landscapes, wildlife
and history. Its present emptiness (parts have less than one person
per ten square miles) belies the fact that in 1750 it supported
almost half the population of Scotland, prior to the clearances and
massive emigration of the later 18th and 19th centuries. Although
the mainland and the Western Isles are characterised by a Celtic
culture and the Gaelic language, the Northern Isles of Shetland
and Orkney demonstrate a powerful association with the Nordic
countries in traditions, music and language.

The Great Glen, running south-west from Inverness and
including Loch Ness, divides the mainland into two distinct parts.
To the west lie the mountains of the North-West Highlands, the
landscape punctuated by isolated peaks such as the spectacular
Suilven (731m/2,399ft) and Canisp (846m/2,779ft) in the
Torridon district with its ancient rocks. In Sutherland, Ben Hope
rises to 927m/3,042ft and Ben Loyal, from the same plateau,
reaches 764m/2,504ft. Much of the northwest Highland coast is
penetrated by long sea lochs such as Loch Torridon, Loch Broom
and Loch Eriboll. The Inner Hebridean island chain includes
mountainous islands such as Skye and Rum and to the west, facing the Atlantic, are the Outer Hebrides comprising Lewis, Harris,
the Uists, and Barra, formed by some of the world's most ancient

rocks. The most spectacular mountains in this archipelago occur on Harris, but everywhere there is a myriad of small lochs, often connected by the narrowest of strips of rocky land. The island systems of Orkney and Shetland to the north of mainland Scotland are quite different, with no mountains and few lochs. Orkney is green and fertile with a tradition of skilful and productive farming, while the poorer peatlands of Shetland have produced more fishermen than farmers. Both have rugged coastlines noted for their vast congregations of seabirds.

To the south-east of the Great Glen and almost overhanging Fort William lies Ben Nevis, at 1,344m/4,406ft Britain's highest mountain. Further east, the broken plateau of the Monadhliaths gives way across the upper Spey to the great grey massif of the Cairngorms, shared with Aberdeenshire. This area contains some of the most extensive native Scots pinewood, relics of the ancient Caledonian Forest which once covered so much of the country. The whole region is noted for its wildlife, from great herds of red deer to still healthy populations of golden eagle and peregrine falcon. The weather records for this region help to dispel a few myths about the Highland climate - the fact, for example, that due to the North Atlantic Drift the average winter temperatures for the north-west are higher than those those of East Anglia, while the Moray coast has some of the highest sunshine records in Scotland. It is true however that rainfall at Fort William is probably the highest for any town in the UK at 2,000mm/78.8in, and it can snow in any month of the year at the higher altitudes of the central Highlands.

Less than one-tenth of the population of the region makes a full-time or even part-time living from the resources of the land and sea, mainly due to the poverty of much of the soil. Increasingly hill sheep farms are being taken over by modern forestry plantations, and to some extent fish farming, which has expanded enormously in recent years, is compensating for the reduction in sea fisheries. Round the Cromarty and Moray Firths, fabrication yards and repair facilities for the oil industry have developed. The fastest-growing sector is tourism. Relative to the rest of the country, the economy of the Highland area has improved and diversified in recent years, partly due to the attraction of new industries to growth centres such as Inverness, and for the first time in more than two centuries, the population has grown in the larger centres with a marked increase in the number of women employed.

Inverness (pop 39,500), located at a strategic point on the intersection of both north-south and east-west routes, can fairly claim to be the capital of the Highlands. It is an ancient settlement site, with an Iron Age vitrified fort at Craig Phadraig, and was visited by St Columba on his successful mission to bring Christianity to the northern Picts. Situated on the River Ness where it flows into the Moray Firth, Inverness found its growth greatly stimulated in the 19th century by the construction of the Caledonian Canal and the coming of the railway. Inverness now houses the headquarters of both the Highland Council, serving the largest catchment area in Britian, and Highland and Island Enterprise, charged with the development of this remote area. This is a focal point for road, rail and air communications in the Northern Highlands – its harbour still supports considerable commercial traffic – and it has seen much recent development as a shopping and distribution centre.

CHAPTER 7

What's in a Name?

Largo, Blebo, Dunino
Into Europe seem to go,
But plainly Scottish we may deem
Auchtermuchty, Pittenweem.

Anon

A PLACE NAME LIKE Auchtermuchty may tease the non-Scottish tongue but, like so many of the place names in Scotland, it has Celtic roots, the first syllable representing the 'upland' and the second, 'swine' – hence 'the high place of the swine'. Pittenweem can be translated as 'the croft by the cave', the 'pit' prefix which is so common on the east coast of Scotland coming from the old British (a form of Gaelic) tongue, often thought to be associated with the Picts, who may have used 'pit' to mean an allotment or share in the land. In the older form of Gaelic, Largo is 'the steep sloping field', while Dunino is 'the fort on the moor'. The prefix 'dun' from the old British, meaning a fort, is very ancient, often known from Iron Age times; Dun-Eidean, from the Welsh Din-eidyn ('fort on a hill face') was the original Edinburgh known to have existed since the third century. Dumfries refers to the fort of the Frisians (people from north of the Weser). Dundee can be translated as 'the south hill fort', but the famed Carse of Gowrie to the west of the city may be from the west Scandinavian 'kjerr' or marsh.

Place names in Scotland come from many different sources, some of which are quite unknown. By far the commonest however are Gaelic names, often modified by English pronunciation and spelling, for example, Gleneagles for Gleann Eaglais ('glen of the church'). The oldest (320BC) place name on record in Scotland is that of Orkney, which is variously translated as 'the tribe of Orcs' (bears) or 'island of seals'. While Tiree was named as the 'land of corn', the opposite was true of the Hebrides: the name means 'islands without corn'. All of the Hebridean islands have Gaelic names, such as Jura, 'island of deer', or Islay, which very aptly translates as 'the divided island' as it is almost in two distinct parts.

The Gaelic name for a mountain, beinn, is often anglicised to the common ben, as in Ben Cruachan, a 'stack-shaped mountain', or Ben Nevis, the 'mountain of dread'. Beinn a Bhuird, one of the peaks rising from the Cairngorm plateau, is the 'table mountain' and to the west of the Cairngorms are the 'grey mountains' – the Monadhliaths. A path or pass is usually 'lairig' in Gaelic, as in Lairig Ghru running through the Cairngorms, the 'awful pass'. The waters that run off the mountains usually have the prefix 'alt', as in Altnaharra, often changed to 'ault' as in Aultroy. Other words for parts of rivers include 'aber', which is old Welsh Gaelic for the outflow, as in Aberdeen (because it was originally confined to Old Aberdeen, this refers not to the outflow of the Dee, but that of the Don). 'Inver' as in Inverness is the inflow of the short River Ness. Names can be quite descriptive, as in Bannockburn, 'shining water', or the Isla, meaning 'gliding water'. Bogs on the other hand are often denoted by 'moine', 'mon' or 'minn', as in Moine Mhor, Monifieth or Minigaff respectively.

Forests are well described in both Gaelic and Norse, perhaps the most memorable being Badnancuileac – 'the thicket infested with midges'! Fetternean – 'wild boar forest' – indicates the loss of our native animals. The Norse for a wood is 'scone', now celebrated in the village of that name outside Perth, and Old English is represented in Shawlands, 'shaw' meaning 'copse' or 'thicket'. Although Gaelic as a spoken language is now confined to the north-west Highlands and Islands, Gaelic place names are common throughout Scotland. Sometimes they are combined with other languages such as Norse, which predominates in the Northern Isles; good examples from Orkney include place names ending in -setter from Norwegian 'saeter' meaning a 'hill farm', or the coastal 'wick' (as in Lerwick in Shetland) from the Norse 'vik' meaning a 'bay' or 'creek'. Many personalised farm names end in 'boll', for example Thorboll meaning 'Thori's farm', or Grimersta meaning 'Grimr's stead' or steading, a common name throughout Scotland for a group of farm buildings. Norse church locations are commemorated in Halkirk in Caithness and Kirkwall in Shetland. More curiously, the Latin for a bishop ('papa') has been retained for many of the Orkney islands such as Papa Westray, after St Boniface.

Compared to Gaelic (including Old British) and Norse, other languages are poorly represented. English names are almost unknown in the Highland area, and occur sparingly in the south, notably between Edinburgh and Berwick. However the oldest known English name in Scotland is Newburgh, on the south bank of the Tay. Elsewhere, the English ending 'ham' indicates a village, as in Whittingham and Coldingham. There are a few 'chesters' (camp) indicating Roman forts, such as Bonchester Bridge in the Borders, and occasional French from the period of Norman settlement, as in Lindsaylands near Biggar, but generally this was too late to affect established place names which had been long established. Cape Wrath from the French 'cap' is relatively modern. The combination of Scots, German and French is demonstrated by my grandmother's instruction to me as a boy to bring back two lamb chops in a pie-dish from the local butcher without letting it fall into the gutter:

"Gang tae the flesher fur twa gigots and tak the ashet (assiette) but dinna let it fa doon the cundie (conduit)"

There is something of a revival of interest in Gaelic, after a period of decline, and now spoken by about 80,000 people, although there are distinct regional speech differences: the Gaelic spoken on either side of the Spey for example, was quite different. Not surprisingly, that language is closely connected to its unique environment and the land; there are extraordinary recorded "songs" emulating, for example, the distinctive call of mother sea-birds encouraging the young to take their first flight from the nest, while the nature poems of the 18th century gamekeeper, Duncan Ban McIntyre, are well known. Names in Gaelic have been given to individual landscape features on the most intimate scale – such as a single tree or small area of bog which had some significance in terms of practical use, historical event, or mythology, so that for example, Carn Eileirg – 'the glen of the deer' – refers to the location of an historic tinchel or trapping area into which the deer were driven.

This level of detailed identification with the land indicates an intimacy with the environment which has largely been lost in modern western society. (It is heartening to note however that in the new heritage centre at Aros near Portree on Skye a tree trail has been established which provides the names of the trees and shrubs in Gaelic) That identification is perhaps best exemplified by the

Gaelic word *dualchas* which combines not only the sense of home and communal heritage, but also something of the individual personality which is bound up with all of these elements, and for which there is no equivalent in English.

CHAPTER EIGHT

The Resourceful Land

We began to take out the boulder stones . . . often after a hard day's work among these stones, with tired muscles and aching hands, I have been unable to enjoy refreshing sleep at night, but in a feverish dream repeated the work of the day.

James Milne – *The Making of a Buchan Farm* (1889)

Looking Back

THE HISTORY OF LAND use in Scotland is a story of increasing control over a hard climate and environment, with the development of technology and improved communications. It starts with the first clearance of the forest for farming in prehistoric times, greatly increased with the help of hard metal tools in the Iron Age, while grazing and fire kept the forest at bay. Agriculture was given a boost from the 12th century onwards by the farming skills of the monastic orders from Europe who were encouraged to settle mainly in the Borders and along the east coast, and a thriving wool trade with the Continent developed during the medieval period. Animal skins became an important export, and there is even a record of 100,000 goat skins being sent to London in one year at the end of the 17th century.

Up to the 1700s farming in Scotland was almost entirely for local subsistence on the 'runrig' system, relics of which can still be seen today. Permanent crops protected from grazing stock were grown on a limited area of 'infield' with the poorer 'outfield' being used for grazing and fuel. Implements were simple and home-made, labour was by families or communal, and much of the diet was based on oatmeal or barley. Until the introduction of crops such as turnips in the 18th century, stock could not be kept through the winter and has to be killed and salted. Summer grazings in the uplands around primitive seasonal shelters known as shielings, used to conserve the infield, persisted well into the 19th century and their remains can still be seen in the moorlands. Fertiliser for the infield was provided by animal manure or seaweed on the coast. The agricultural landscape was open and unenclosed.

The agricultural revolution of the 18th century was greatly assisted by extensive enclosure of fields, providing for systematic crop rotation and integration of livestock and arable crops. Improvement in the land such as the removal of stones, draining and fertilising were encouraged by the longer leases granted by landowners to farming tenants. In the Highlands, there was a massive increase in cattle trade to feed the British army and navy, and to supply the needs of rapidly expanding towns, while the recently introduced potato displaced grain as a diet staple. During this period and subsequently, large-scale reclamation of wasteland was undertaken, often by the removal of huge quantities of stones and peat by hand, such as in north-east Aberdeenshire, the Carse of Stirling and Strathmore, to create some of the richest farming lands in the country.

The improvement in communications and transport changed the farming economy, with the development of rural markets and specialised agricultural trades such as blacksmiths, saddlers (horses replacing oxen as draught animals) and cart-makers. Farming specialisation became commoner and rural industries such as spinning, weaving and quarrying attracted work forces to the many small towns which developed as satellites of the larger industrial centres. The basic structure of the landscape, with large enclosed fields associated with individual isolated farms (unlike the village communities of England) laid out in the agricultural revolution of the 18th and 19th centuries is still the typical pattern of lowland Scottish countryside today.

The late 18th and 19th centuries also saw the introduction of large flocks of southern Blackface and Cheviot sheep into the Highlands; sheep farmers were able to pay higher rents than the local people, who were forced off the land in the notorious Clearances. Many of the inland glen communities were obliged to settle on the less hospitable coast to develop the fishing industry and provide labour for the very profitable gathering of kelp, which apart from its industrial use, was a rich source of fertiliser. This emigration established the pattern of today's crofting townships in the west Highlands and Islands, with houses frequently straggling alongside a coastal road.

Although in 1750 the population north of the Tay was as great as that to the south, a century and a half later emigration had reduced the highland area to a largely depopulated land. As a result of changes from subsistence to cash farming, increases in efficiency and the drift to the towns, the numbers engaged in agriculture in Scotland dropped from 500,000 to 200,000 during the 19th century. Cheap grain and wool from the Empire in the latter half of that century depressed prices for these commodities, and in the Highland area encouraged the replacement of sheep by deer. Victorian industrialists, mainly from the south, took advantage of the favourable land prices and their new-found wealth to establish vast hunting estates for deer-stalking and grouse-shooting, and this form of land use is still dominant over much of the Highlands today. Around the reoccupied castles and shooting lodges, there was much exotic tree planting for landscape and amenity purposes, producing the mature policy woodlands characteristic of many of Scotland's large country estates.

Farming in 20th century Scotland has been revolutionised by mechanisation, intensification and the use of chemicals. The first tractors appeared before World War I, and the first combine harvester was tried in 1932. In 1938 there were 146,000 horses on Scottish farms, reduced to 20,000 in 1960. I can recall not only working with horses both on farms and in the forest in Angus in the mid-1950's, but also seeing them used quite regularly as draft animals in the streets of Dundee not long before this. World War II gave a boost to Scottish agriculture, following the depressions of the 1920s and 1930s, and there has been a progressive enlargement of farms and specialisation since then, utilising new crop varieties and stock breeds. In recent years, industrial forestry has taken the place of sheep farming over much of the uplands, and European Community quotas and regulations have increasingly determined farming structures and economics. The average cost of agricultural land in 1995 was approximately £1000 per hectare/ 2.5 acres for hill and upland and £2000 for low ground.

Farming Today

Six days shalt thou labour
And do all that thou art able
On the Sabbath day wash the horses' legs
And tidy up the stable.

Anon

With the end of horse-power on Scottish farms over 30 years ago this 'Ploughman's Commandment' seems archaic, but it still reflects the commitment of Scottish farmers to the land and their stock under very changed circumstances. Given its environment, Scottish agriculture is one of the most efficient in Europe, and the country is self-sufficient in temperate food-stuffs. The quality of Scottish agricultural and fish products is renowned, from salmon to Scotch beef and lamb. There is a clear distinction between farming in the uplands, which predominate over much of the country, and the arable lowlands, largely confined to the central belt and the coastal plain. Indeed, there are over 38,000 square kilometres/ 14,000 square miles classed as "rough grazing" compared with only 41 square kilometres/17 square miles in the Class 1 category i.e. land of the highest agricultural quality. In the east of Scotland, from Banffshire to Berwickshire, low rainfall and rich soils favour crops such as barley, wheat, potatoes and vegetables. The wetter west, especially the south-west, is the best for grass to support milk production and dairy products.

The hill land is important for the breeding of sheep and cattle, usually fed on hay or straw bought from lowland farms. Low-ground farmers often finish the stock-rearing process by feeding cattle and sheep bought in the spring and autumn from hill farms. Regional specialities include the soft-fruit industry of Tayside (in my own school holidays, rows of raspberries to be picked seemed endless, not surprising as this area is the largest for this fruit in Western Europe), notably in Strathmore and the Carse of Gowrie, and the famed early potatoes of the Ayrshire coast. The colder climate of Scotland can be beneficial in reducing disease and insect attack in seed potatoes for example. There has been a progressive change in recent years from mixed farming to speciality farming which, combined with field enlargement, has reduced the variety of the farming scene in the lowlands.

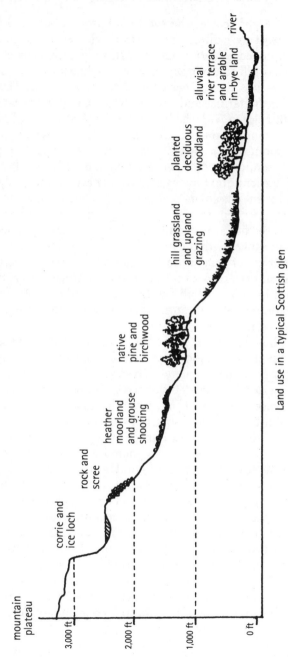

Land use in a typical Scottish glen

mountain
plateau

corrie and
ice loch

rock and
scree

heather
moorland
and grouse
shooting

native
pine and
birchwood

hill grassland
and upland
grazing

planted
deciduous
woodland

alluvial
river terrace
and arable
in-bye land

river

3,000 ft

2,000 ft

1,000 ft

0 ft

Some 76 per cent of the total land area of Scotland is under some form of agricultural production. However, the number of people employed on farms has been steadily decreasing and in the last 10 years full time employment has reduced by over one third to 29,000 – less than 2 per cent of the population – frequently made up of the farmer and his family. As a boy in the late 1940's

I recall helping with the harvest on an Angus farm binding by hand and standing on end the sheaves of oats which we called 'stooks', alongside a dozen other farm workers. Despite the undoubted importance of the primary industries to the Scottish economy, agriculture, forestry and fishing account for only 4.4 per cent of all rural employment, compared to 70 per cent in services and over 17 per cent in manufacturing. There are 30,500 agricultural units, the highest percentage being in the 20 - 100 hectare/50 – 250 acres range, with the north-west of the country having double the average of smaller units under 20 hectares/50 acres in the crofting counties (10 per cent of all land is under the crofting system, about one third of all Scottish farm holdings). Average farm size in Scotland is now larger than in any other region of the European Community.

There has been a net loss of agricultural land over the last 10 years, ranging from 9,000 to 42,000 hectares each year, by far the highest proportion to upland forestry – in 1985 this reached a peak of 24,000 hectares/60,000acres, falling to just over 8,000 hectares/20,000 acres in 1995. Even this lower figure is ten times greater than losses to industry, housing and roads, the next most important source of loss. In European terms, 86 per cent of agricultural land in Scotland is designated as Least Favoured Area, reflecting the low proportion of good arable land.

At the same time, agricultural incomes have fluctuated markedly – from £25 million in 1985 to £537 million in 1995, when there was almost a doubling of income over the preceding 2 years, but falling back by 18 percent in 1996 for example. In the designated Least Favoured Areas, mainly in the uplands, a high proportion of that income is derived from subsidy – the Hill Livestock Compensatory Allowance rose from £39 million in 1996 to £63 million in 1997. The net worth of Scottish agriculture rose from £6,000 million in 1986 to £8,000 million in 1995.

Crops

Oats are the cereal most closely associated with the Scots diet of the past, but the most widespread grain crop now grown is barley, partly for feeding livestock, and partly to provide the main ingredient for whisky and beer – high-quality malting barley is a speciality of Scotland. Wheat is also grown in limited areas, either for cattle feed or for making bread, and oats are now coming back into favour as a breakfast cereal or for feeding to horses, although at 150,000 tonnes per annum, the crop is less than a quarter of wheat production. Grass crops are important for cattle and sheep feed, often made into silage, which has doubled in production in the last 10 years. A wide range of vegetables are grown, mainly in the central lowlands, with tomatoes and other salad crops grown under glass concentrated in the Clyde Valley. More than half the total potato crop is grown for seed. Turnip is important as winter animal feed. The newest crop is the brilliant yellow oil seed rape which colours the countryside in June and is used for oil extraction for cooking and lubrication.

Cultivated arable land amounts to 667,000ha/1,648,160 acres with a further 1,035,000ha/2,557,485 acres of cultivable land. The proportion of cultivated land varies from 2.7 per cent in the north west to over 32 per cent in the north east. In 1996 cereal production rose by 9 per cent to a total of 2.9 million tonnes, with a staggering increase in barley production of 37 per cent between 1994 and 1995.

A typical lowland arable farm in East Lothian may be 200ha/ 494 acres in extent, run by the farmer and one assistant, under a highly efficient and mechanised system. Most of the land near the coast is under 50m/150ft in altitude, well drained and fertile, with no steep slopes to create problems for machines. Rainfall in this part of East Lothian is likely to be around 600mm/24in per annum, which makes it one of the driest places in Britain. About 10 per cent of the farm may be in winter barley, 10 per cent in oil seed rape, 10 per cent in peas likely to be grown on contract for a freezing firm, while more than 60 per cent of the farm may be used for winter wheat, planted in the autumn to mature the following summer. The high proportion of wheat is justified by its high production compared to barley, but continued cropping of this cereal on the same fields is dependent on high fertiliser input and effective spraying against weeds and pests. On a rocky volcanic outcrop, the remaining 10 per cent is permanent grass to provide grazing for 40 beef cows and their calves, supplemented by surplus hay from the arable crop. About 40 calves will be sold each April to other farmers who have more grass to fatten them.

Livestock

Scottish livestock is internationally renowned for quality and hardiness, especially its beef cattle, dairy cows and sheep providing breeding stock throughout the U.K and overseas. While the Aberdeen Angus is still a byword for beef quality, there has been substantial introduction of new cattle breeds from Europe, such as Simmental, Limousin and Charolais. The total annual consumption of beef per head of population is approximately 20 kg/44lb. The main dairy breeds are Ayrshire, Friesian and Holstein, with 20 per cent of the calves going into beef production. Friesian and Friesian-Ayrshire crosses now form 80 per cent of the dairy herd, replacing the traditional pure Ayrshire dairy cow. In 1990 the average consumption of milk in Scotland was just over 2.24 litres/4 pints per person per week.

There are almost a million beef cattle and over 9 million sheep (1996). Among the mountain and upland sheep, the most popular is the Blackface with its capacity to survive hard Scottish winters, but it is increasingly crossed with the Cheviot for better production and finer wool. The lambs are usually fattened on lowland farms where the Scottish Greyface and half breeds are common. Scotland provides over one quarter (3.5 million) of the breeding ewes in the UK.

Because of climatic conditions and quality of feed, hill and mountain ewes in Scotland seldom have more than one lamb per year, whereas on lowland farms twins and triplets are common. Together with pigs and poultry, usually reared intensively under cover, the value of Scottish livestock and livestock products is over £1,000 million.

A typical dairy farm in the south-west of Scotland may be 80ha/ 200 acres in extent, and, if below 100m/300ft, is likely to have moderately good, well drained soils in undulating country, with an average of 1000 mm/39 in of rain each year. It is likely that as a result of milk quotas, the number of dairy cows will have been reduced by one fifth to less than 100. Up to 100 per cent of the farm may be improved by drainage, fertilising and re-seeding. Farms at higher altitudes may have poorer, peaty soils, and there is likely to be an increase in the proportion of beef cattle and possibly some sheep to make use of this. Dairy cows require milking twice a day, and on average produce milk for four to five years, for ten months each year following the birth of a calf. Calving is either in spring or autumn, and the herd is kept indoors over the winter and fed on silage and concentrates.

Commercial hill sheep farming has been an important part of the Scottish agricultural scene for over 200 years. It was highly profitable from the late 18th century onwards, and there are records of over 200,000 sheep passing through the autumn markets of Falkirk in 1827, along with 130,000 cattle. It was given a particular boost by the boom in exports of carpets in the mid 19th century while wool prices were increasing as a result of the shutdown in imports of cotton during the American Civil War. However, with the import of mutton and wool from Australia in the new refrigerated ships from the early 1870s onwards, domestic prices declined sharply and the industry has seen big market fluctuations since then, with virtual collapse in hill farming generally in the 1980s. There are very clear differences between regions in the proportions of land dedicated to rough grazing - the north east has approximately half that of the north west. There is now very little commercial sheep farming in the north-west Highlands, although throughout Scotland about 75 percent of the larger estates still carry at least reduced sheep stocks. Rough hill grazing including shared grazing covers 4,033,000ha/9,965,543 acres.

There is a very close interconnection between hill sheep farms and low-ground farms. The hill farms supply good quality disease-free lambs to improve low-ground stock, with the crossing of hill-bred tups with low-ground ewes, while the low ground can provide the better feed for finishing lambs prior to sale. The same farms may provide over-wintering ground or the hay and other crops required by the hill farmer who has sufficient in-bye (improved and enclosed low ground fields) to keep his stock over the winter. The crucial equation is the amount of available winter feed relative to the amount of summer hill ground, since the latter is usually in excess, even although the actual summer growth period on the heights may be as little as six weeks. Ewes are now often fed in winter to improve lambing rates, but after five to six years of lambing they will be brought down to the less rigorous conditions of the low ground to lamb for a few more years.

On average, sheep numbers on the hill farm double during the summer on the upland grass, to be reduced to the original number before winter. Lambing is undoubtedly the busiest time of the year for any hill farmer, although it has been made easier by all-terrain hill vehicles and motor cycles, and the increasing trend towards bringing sheep off the hill for the lambing period. Stock are moved off the low ground in the spring to allow for grass growth for mowing later in the summer, and to utilise the hill grazings. Some hill farms grow their own root crops to boost stock feed in early winter. There are usually at least two dippings of the sheep to reduce diseases and pests. In summer clipping takes place, now requiring much less labour than previously – wool prices in recent years have dropped to the point where it is barely economic to clip. The summer lamb sales in August – more than 30,000 lambs will be handled in a day at the Lairg sales in Sutherland – and the later sales of old ewes and breeding tups will tell the hill farmer whether it has been a good or bad year, before the quieter winter period. However, bad weather especially long lying snow drifts, can cause great anxiety; whole flocks can suffocate unless the shepherd can trace them and dig them out.

It is reckoned that one man can adequately look after 800 ewes, but in recent years there has been a tendency to put more sheep on the land than it can stand, including ground usually grazed by deer: agricultural land used for sheep does not attract rates whereas sporting ground is subject to this taxation. In some areas of Scotland, up to 50 per cent of the hill farms have an income of less than £10,000 per year, which is one reason why shepherd's offspring are not following in their parents' footsteps.

The farming of red deer is a newer livestock development, primarily for the production of venison, much of which is exported to Europe, although prices have fallen considerably in recent years. Originally from wild stock, the deer require to be enclosed by high fences to prevent escape.

Organic farming represents a minute proportion of the total farming enterprise in Scotland. There remains the disparity in the the relatively higher shop prices for such products, which is partly due to the economies of scale of non-organic farming. Truly sustainable farming, with its massive reduction in external inputs of energy and other resources, would represent a wholesale revolution in attitudes and technologies which does not seem to be a realistic prospect in the forseeable future, however desirable. As in other areas however, apart from a significant change in public demand, any substantial increase in the costs of such items as fuel and chemicals would be most likely to push farming systems in this direction.

The Disappearing Forest

From the bank of the Tweed to St Andrews I had never seen a single tree which
I did not believe to have grown up far within the present century ... a tree might
be a show in Scotland as a horse in Venice.

Samuel Johnson – *A Journey to the Western Islands* (1775)

By Neolithic times, substantial areas of the original native forests which once clothed much of Scotland had been cleared, and the subsequent centuries reduced this to a few relics. Extensive grazing by domestic stock ensured that regrowth of the forest was confined to the few areas inaccessible to these animals, and constant burning to encourage grass for grazing combined to produce the open moorland and hill landscapes of today In the west, large areas of natural oak woodland were managed for charcoal production for iron smelting and tannin for curing leather, but became derelict when these systems were replaced by more modern processes. Extensive areas of prime woodland were felled to provide timber for shipbuilding, notably for the navy. The evidence for the great extent of the original forest can be found in the remains of many trees preserved in deep peat bogs.

Although decrees to protect the royal hunting forests were made from early medieval times onwards, serious attempts at tree planting had to wait until the 18th century. The so-called 'planting lairds' of central and west Scotland beautified their estates with introduced tree species often brought back by Scots explorers and botanists, specifically sent to collect tree seed for this purpose. The most successful of these species came from western North America, especially the Pacific Coast ranges, where climatic and soil conditions are not dissimilar to those of Scotland. These include the well-known Douglas fir and Norway spruce, but it is the sitka spruce from British Columbia which is the predominant tree in Scotland's modern commercial conifer plantations. European larch, our only deciduous conifer, was also extensively planted from this time. Nevertheless, by the end of the 19th century, the forest area was at an all-time low, probably covering not more than 300,000ha/750,000acres.

The New Forests

Two World Wars took a heavy toll of the remaining timber resources of Scotland, but with the establishment of the Forestry Commission in 1919 extensive reafforestation was begun, including the planting of some of the great sand dune systems of Culbin on the Moray Firth and later, Tentsmuir on the Fife Coast. The greatest expansion has occurred since 1960, and the rate of planting in the 20 years since then has meant that large areas of conifer forest are of a similar age. Some of the largest artificial forests are in Galloway, the Central Borders and Argyll, including Mull. Unlike the Scandinavian countries, in Scotland there has been little tradition of small-scale forestry carried out by farmers, partly due to tenure conditions and the linking of forestry with estate rights, including sporting use.

Large-scale industrial forestry has resulted in the most obvious change in the Scottish countryside in the last 70 years – between the 1940s and the 1970s there was a 328 per cent increase in conifer planting (dominated by sitka spruce and lodgepole pine) raising the proportion of land under woodland from 7.2 percent in 1947 to 12.6 per cent in 1995, i.e. less than half the average (25 per cent) for other European Union countries. This has only been made possible by such important developments as the deep forestry plough which has carved through the great peatlands of the north and west and broken up the compacted iron layer in these acid soils.

New mechanical draining techniques, the application of chemicals as fertiliser and for weed control, and genetic improvements in treestock, have all combined to give the forester far greater control of the inhospitable hill environment of Scotland where most planting has been carried out. The productive woodland area is about 12 per cent, of which 92 per cent is conifer plantation, while there is a much higher proportion of broadleaved woodland in the private sector compared with state forestry. Some 30 per cent of the land is unsuitable for tree crops, and all of the available good forestry land has already been taken up for this purpose. A real concern in these new plantations is the high risk of extensive wind damage especially on shallow soils in exposed situations.

This land, whether heather moorland or grassland, was previously used for hill sheep farming or gamesport such as grouse-shooting or deer-stalking. Exposure limits these plantations to an average upper altitude of about 500m/1500ft in the south, falling to 300m/1,000 ft in the more exposed west. Some 68 per cent of all new conifer planting in Britain is located in Scotland, where the total area of such forests is over

1,000,000ha/2,500,000 acres in both state and private ownership. Soil, climate and terrain often provide good conditions for forestry, and growth rates for conifers in particular are considerably higher than in other forest areas in Europe. Scotland has almost 50 per cent of the total productive woodland and provides about a third of all industrial wood in Great Britain: in 1995 it produced 3.5 million cubic metres/123 million cubic feet of timber, with a value of £97 million. Direct employment in the forestry industry is estimated at 12,000, although the staff employed by the Forestry Commission is progressively declining and now stands at around 3,500.

An obvious but important distinction between farming and forestry is the period before harvest – 40 years for coniferous species, while deciduous woodlands may have a rotation of between 100 and 200 years. However the risk of wind-throw to shallow-rooted conifers such as sitka spruce, combined with the labour costs of thinning plantations, favours early felling for pulp-wood. This has important implications for the ecological development of the forest, since it is usually the maturer woodlands which have been progressively thinned that are the most attractive both for wildlife and amenity. Whereas farming can take account of rapid changes in technology, economics or even public attitudes, this is much more difficult under the longer-term planning required in forestry. The layout and management of plantations established 30 years ago may not be appropriate today, and this applies to changes in public perception of landscape and wildlife values of plantation forestry in the 1990s.

Mechanisation has dramatically changed forestry operations from the days of hand axe and cross-cut saw which I recall using in the woods of Angus in the early 1950's: some 20-40 trees a day can be cut with a single chain-saw, while the old-fashioned 'snedding' of side branches has given way to mechanised de-branching and even cross-cutting by a single machine. On steep slopes, horse extraction has been replaced by cables which can take out 100 tonnes of timber a week, and even felling can be carried out by a machine that both cuts trees and stacks the timber. Application of fertiliser around the time of planting is most often carried out by helicopters, but planting remains one forestry task which has still to be carried out by hand, cutting a notch in the bank of soil created by the deep ploughs which carve swathes through the peat. On all but the gentlest slopes this ploughing is done across the contours for the safety of the operator, to reduce the risk of overturning, a technique which may increase the risk of soil erosion on the steeper slopes. A competent worker can plant 25-30ha/62.5-85 acres a day in the planting season between the end of February and mid-May. Before this the land will have been fenced against sheep, in which case the fence need only be 0.9-1.2m/3-4ft in height – the 1.8m/6ft fences seen more often in the north and west are to prevent access by deer.

With the sale of state forests (in 1996 just under 4,000 ha were offered for sale) and the encouragement given to private forestry, the rate of planting in the private sector is approximately double that of the Forestry Commission. Broadleaf forestry is a much smaller, but increasing, percentage at about 90,000 hectares. This is still less than 1 per cent of the total of 13.5 per cent of the land area of Scotland occupied by productive forest. The present rate of planting is about 13,000ha/32,500 acres annually for both conifers and broadleaf species, by far the greatest proportion now being carried out by private estates. With new incentives for farm woodlands, and the prospect of the setting aside of more arable land to control agricultural production in Europe, it is possible that more forestry will take place on the better, lower ground, offering the opportunity to grow a wider range of species with better potential timber quality.

Forests, Wildlife and People

There is considerable argument about the pro's and con's of modern forestry as it affects the environment and amenity of the Scottish landscape. There is no doubt that large single-species plantations, often planted at one time so that there is little variation in the age and size of the closely spaced trees, are an inhibiting environment for wildlife. For walkers and others, such dense plantations can obscure views, are difficult to penetrate except via standard forestry roads, and present a monotonous appearance. Deep ploughing and forest drains can increase local flooding and affect salmon and trout spawning grounds by washing down sediments. Large blocks of closed forest substantially reduce the feeding grounds of predatory birds such as golden eagle and raven. In areas with granitic rocks, such as the Cairngorms and western Galloway, large-scale coniferous tree planting has increased the acidity of lochs and rivers, some of which have become fishless.

The other side of the coin is that fencing out of both domestic stock (especially sheep) and deer has reduced over-grazing, at least within the forest. As a result, until the young trees shade out the light, natural vegetation can recover and provide sanctuary for small mammals such as voles, stoats and ground-nesting birds. Woodland birds are attracted to the new forest, and the increase in distribution of the wild cat is most likely to be because of the extensive cover provided by new plantations. In some areas, roe deer have increased to the point where they have become serious pests. Because game-keeping has been reduced, species previously considered vermin can thrive. The forests have become important recreation areas where positive access is provided for walkers, bikers, fishermen and casual picnickers. Careful landscaping of the more recent plantations and increasing provision for wildlife habitat is making public forestry more acceptable in Scotland, and it is clear that this activity will be more positively planned and managed in future for a wider range of uses rather than solely timber production.

Native woodlands in Scotland form less than 1 per cent of the land, with 90 per cent of this in the Highlands, mostly pine and birch. Some 2,700 ha/6,670 acres have been planted under the new native pinewood scheme and management for regeneration has been carried out on a further 1,460 ha/3606 acres, so that, together with specially protected areas for this species, the future for native Scots pinewood is more secure than it has been for centuries. Enhanced grants for native broadleaved species have given a boost to their planting on both hill and low ground, and it would be true to say that both the state and private sector have considerably altered their approach to forestry for conservation over the last decade, prompted by increasing public pressure.

The Sea's Harvest

You would have thought that all the boats belonging to Scotland had been off Peterhead last night – the sea was literally covered by boats ... we were obliged to go at quarter speed to guard against collision.

Charles Weld – *Two Months in the Highlands* (1860)

This picture of a thriving fishing industry, based largely on the huge quantities of herring taken in the latter half of the 18th and beginning of the 19th century, is in stark contrast to the sadly depleted Scottish fishing fleet of today, now numbering less than 4,000 vessels of all sizes. Although sea fisheries are still important, with the value of the fish landed in Scotland in 1995 at over £200 million, the herring fishery virtually collapsed in the 1970s, and its North Sea fishery was closed in 1977 due to shortage of fish: in 1995 the value of the herring landings was under £10 million, considerably less than a fifth of that for the most valuable, haddock, at £50 million, although this was £5 million below the value in the previous year. There are just over 8,000 fishermen employed on a full-time or part-time basis. The purse seine net has displaced trawl netting and this, together with high technology equipment, including sonar for detecting fish shoals, has made fishing more efficient, unfortunately to the considerable detriment of fish stocks. Now Scottish fishermen are threatened with enforced tie-up of their expensive vessels (a typical modern fishing vessel can cost £0.5 million) and decommissioning schemes are proposed by the government.

Peterhead has overtaken Aberdeen as largest fishing port, and these two account for just over half of all Scottish landings haddock, cod and whiting. The main port for herring and mackerel is Ullapool - mackerel catches have increased considerably in recent years, a high proportion being transhipped direct from Scottish catchers' boats to the buyers' processing vessels, often from Russia and East Europe. The main fishing grounds lie west of Orkney and Shetland, although there are important concentrations in the Minch, around the Hebrides and off the north Buchan Coast. This is also the location of the sand eel fishery which in the 1980s was landing in excess of 60000 tonnes of fish, mainly used for stock feed (including farmed salmon); questions have been raised about its possible effect on the important sea bird populations in the area. Another source of dispute is the effect of seals on fishing catches – the estimated minimum population of grey seals is over 105,000 with at least a further 26,000 common seals.

Salmon and sea trout are also fished commercially – the annual total including those caught by rod line, amounts to approximately 17,000 salmon and 60,000 sea trout – commanding high prices both for the wild fish and sporting rentals. Atlantic salmon are also caught, mainly off the east coast of Scotland by fixed net or 'engines', as they are known, which are strictly controlled by law. These include bag net, fly net or, on sandy shores, stake nets. The only legal moving net system which can be employed inside an estuary is by and cable (rowing boat). Monofilament nets were banned in 1962.

Farming for Fish

Scotland is ideally placed for the development of one of its newest industries: fish farming. It has abundant high-quality freshwater required for hatcheries and early growth stages, long sheltered sea lochs for subsequent on-growing, strong tidal flows necessary to bring in constant supplies of clean water, and temperatures in Scottish coastal waters, warmed by the North Atlantic Drift on the west coast, are relatively high. It also has a tradition of fishing and boat handling which provides many of the skills required. Fin fish farming (i.e. excluding shell fish) includes both inland freshwater trout farms and, more importantly, Atlantic salmon rearing in both freshwater and saltwater phases over the five years from egg hatching to mature fish development. As long ago as 1987, production from salmon farms had reached about twelve times the combined total catch by rod and net.

Scotland is now the second-largest producer of Atlantic

salmon in the world, and a high proportion of salmon and trout sold in the UK now come from Scottish fish farms, although many of these are owned by Norwegian companies. With some 580 registered salmon sites alone, there is hardly a sea loch on the west coast that does not support one or more such enterprise, although recent drops in fish prices have forced closure of a number of these. Production of salmon in 1996 was 83,000 tonnes, double what it was in 1992, and this is predicted to rise to 132,000 tonnes by the end of the century. Scottish salmon has a world-wide reputation, and £200 million worth was exported in 1996. The industry, covering all forms of fish farming, employs 2,000 people directly (1,000 in full-time jobs) and an additional 10,000 in processing and distributing making a valuable contribution to local employment in remote areas; it is worth more than £100 million per annum to the Highlands and Islands region, which justifies the investment of over £15 million by Highlands and Islands Enterprise.

It is an industry involving considerable scientific research and utilising modern technology, including for example the use of helicopters to transport young fish in special oxygenated containers from hatcheries to pens to reduce stress to a minimum. Most salmon-rearing is carried out west of the Great Glen, since the hatcheries are usually situated close to Highland rivers for the volume of fresh water required, while the sea pens are concentrated on the west coast and in Shetland. This intensive rearing of farmed fish has created some concern about its impact on such environments. Although the industry claims that all farm pens in Scotland occupy no more than 100ha/250 acres (the size of a small land-based farm) they are often located in the areas of greatest scenic and ecological value in the whole of Scotland. There is danger to the water quality of lochs and rivers from effluents containing both organic matter and chemicals including antibiotics harmful to other life. Anxieties have been expressed about the transfer of disease to wild stock, but the most serious concern is the real possibility of loss of the genetic variety of wild salmon through interbreeding and competition from the increasing number of farmed fish now found in the open as a result of escapes from cages or dumping.

With a 1995 value of over £87 million, shellfish have become an increasingly important part of the Scottish seafood industry, much of which now comes from farmed produce. There is a ready international market for this high-quality product, mainly lobster, scallops and mussels, but also including crab and oyster. At the present time there are about 350 shellfish farms in Scotland concentrated on the west coast and the islands, including Orkney and Shetland. In their own interests, shell fish farmers are most concerned to maintain a pollution free environment for their stocks which can be affected by fin fish farming activities.

Gamesport

The beautiful rolling moorlands are the home of feathered game, while up in the mountains red deer run wild, feasting on moss and lichen. The higher you climb in search of them the sweeter will be the venison....here too is the home of the mountain hare...plump trout and other fish inhabit the fathomless lochs and unpolluted burns while salmon leap their way majestically up river....

Jean Warren – *A Feast of Scotland* 1979

Land dedicated to gamesport still occupies substantial areas of Scotland both north and south of the Highland line.With the arrival of feudalism in the 11th and 12th centuries, medieval hunting forests were specially protected for the Royal hunts which included wild boar and wolf as well as deer – the latter were protected from hunting in snowstorms for example. The first legislation relating to salmon was passed in 1318 and in 1474 strict laws were passed by James III to protect raptors, no doubt for falconry. In 1535 a third offence of woodcutting in protected areas meant execution. However there was no relationship between the right to hunt and land ownership: any free person could hunt, and the game that was killed belonged to that person. Over the centuries, hunting became increasingly associated with land ownership rights, which is still the position today. Legislation has progressively limited the methods, seasons and species that can be hunted. Agricultural and crofting tenants have however retained the legal right from the 1880s to control animals causing serious damage to their crops.

The destruction of the forest converted the red deer from a woodland animal to a much lighter, faster hill grazer, unlike its cousin in the Continental forests. A herd of Scottish red deer moving at speed apparently without effort over the roughest ground is a remarkable sight – even running uphill, they seem to float across the heather and peat bog. Deer stalking as a sport was introduced by the Duke of Bedford as late as 1818: before that deer would be hunted with hounds and often driven into cul-de-sac glens or enclosures. There are records of deer parks being established to maintain a ready source of venison; an instruction was sent to one of the Duke of Montrose's keepers on Loch Lomondside in the mid-16th century 'to kill two fat bucks as his Majesty and his Gentlemen will be visiting the island (Inchmurrin) and they are sure to have sharp stomachs'. It was the decline of the great sheep runs that led to the creation of the great sporting estates by southern industrial magnates between 1870 and 1910. By the 1860s, sporting rentals for the first time exceeded those for sheep, and between 1880 and 1906 sheep numbers dropped by 30 per cent.

Queen Victoria's consort, Prince Albert, was a keen sportsman and helped to make Highland hunting fashionable. By the 1880s some 4,500 red deer stags were being shot each year on Highland estates. Big landowners, such as the Duke of Sutherland, obliged the new railway companies to build railway stations for the convenience of shooting guests as a condition of permission to allow the development of lines across their land. Considerable antagonism was aroused in a number of cases by the complete exclusion of public access and the ferocity with which poachers were prosecuted. (Modern commercial poaching, especially at night, is still apparently prevalent; animals are often taken in poor condition and wounded animals left to die slowly.) Despite changing fortunes and death duties, many of these stalking estates still exist, often under foreign ownership; in the west, deer forest has virtually replaced grouse moor, with an attendant marked decline in grouse numbers. The shooting lodges, many built in elaborate 'Scots baronial' style with their planted driveways and amenity woodlands, remain a distinctive if anomalous feature of the Highland landscape.

The stag-shooting season lasts from 1 July to 20 October, while hinds can be shot from 21 October to 15 February. The roaring of stags during the October rutting season echoing through a Highland glen is a highly evocative sound. It is claimed that trophy hunting hardly exists, and that the aim is to maintain the quality of the stock by taking out the poorer animals. Telescopic rifle sights have largely replaced older 'open' sights, so that with an experienced stalker to lead the shooter there is much less likelihood of animals being wounded. Stag shooting requires considerably less skill than grouse shooting, but the culling of hinds, often in poor weather, is usually the work of professional stalkers. The practice of bringing the shot animals off the hill by pony ('garron') has largely been replaced by vehicle transport. Deer can move across estate boundaries where the land is unfenced, but in a number of cases they are fed in winter, which habituates them to particular areas; forestry fencing can also force the deer on to lower ground where they can cause damage to crops or wander on to roads. Until recently, Scottish venison commanded high prices on the Continent, with the trend towards consumption of lean meat, but the fall in price in the 1990s has undermined this source of estate income.

Grouse shooting had become so popular in the latter half of the 19th century that by the 1880s some 500,000 red grouse were being shot in the Highlands alone each year. What is not in dispute is that the popularity of grouse shooting resulted in the systematic destruction of any creature, animal or bird, which was likely to reduce the number of the quarry species, confirmed by the appalling detailed records in game books of "vermin killed" – a number of species were completely eliminated. It is claimed with some justification that the natural history of the Highlands has not yet recovered either from this slaughter, or from the burning and very intensive sheep grazing over the last 200 years. While the maintenance of a proportion of grouse moor by burning contributes to the overall diversity of habitats, it is a form of monoculture, and it is questionable whether vast tracts set aside for this purpose are in the best interests of conservation.

The attraction of the grouse for the sportsman is its speed of flight, which can reach 113kmph/70mph, and the quickness of action required when a covey is being driven at speed over the butts - the cairns of stones or turf which can be seen at intervals along the moorland slopes, behind which the shooters stand. (With other youngsters, my recollection is of aching muscles resulting from 'beating' the grouse through knee high heather towards these butts for days at a time) Traditionally the grouse season starts on the 'Glorious Twelfth' (12 August) and ends on 10 December. Grouse numbers can fluctuate widely, and a cold wet spring can be lethal to the young birds, many of which, especially if a second brood is raised, will be too young to shoot by the opening of the season. The keepers will try to remove older birds later in the season to maintain the youngest potential breeders and keep predation to a minimum; estates that used to maintain a team of keepers mainly for this purpose are often now reduced to a single employee who is hard pressed to keep up with all the tasks assigned to him. Unfortunately the less scrupulous also persecute protected species of predatory birds for this reason, and there is no doubt that some species have never recovered from the mass slaughter on the Scottish hills in earlier decades. In order to maintain grouse stocks there are now calls for the removal from the protected list of certain predatory birds which are only now recovering from their former decimation

In 1914 deer forest covered some 14,000sq km/5,405sq miles, but the expansion of forestry in particular has reduced this considerably. The decline in gamekeeping after World War II signalled the end of the shooting heyday, and since 1930 there has been a rapid decline in grouse numbers, from an average of 40 birds per square kilometre to half that or less at the present time, partly as a result of disease and the ravages of the heather beetle. Heather moorland, its summer purple colour so characteristic of the eastern uplands of Deeside, Speyside, Perthshire and Angus, was reduced by 29 per cent as a result of changes in land use in the 30 years following World War II. Because of the manpower involved, and the extension of forestry, it is no longer easy to carry out the periodic burning that is essential to maintain the various ages of heather for a good grouse moor. This practice, often puzzling to the visitor, creates the striped pattern of recently burnt patches on many Scottish hillsides. Great care is required to burn under the right conditions – hot fires on dry ground can get into the underlying peatland burn for a very long time, with risk of serious erosion, especially on the steeper slopes. Much heather moorland has been reclaimed or converted into grassland by intensive sheep grazing and uncontrolled burning.

The extent of gamesport use can be gauged from recent annual shooting figures for red deer at nearly 60,000 (including stags, hinds and calves), nearly 13,000 other deer species, over 1 million pheasants, over 250,000 grouse and 100,000 ducks with other gamebird species bringing the total to over 1.5 million. It is estimated that this brings in revenue of £28.6 million to the estate economy, and a very similar amount from provision of services such as food, accommodation, equipment sales and so on. It is reckoned to support over 2,000 full-time jobs and a further 11,000 part-time jobs. Within the tourist economy, the sporting visitors (often from overseas) are among the highest spenders. A recent estimate for the salmon and trout fishery in Scotland gave a value of over £50 million, although it is now clear that there is considerable loss to the Scottish salmon fishery from drift netting (banned in Scotland) off the Northumbrian coast. The marked – and on many rivers, disastrous – decline in salmon catches this century has paralleled that for grouse bags and contrasts with the rise in red deer numbers. These marked population changes could indicate serious environmental effects, from different sources, on the quality of land and water in our hill country.

The capital value of sporting estates for sale is usually based on, among other things, the notional value of the available game for shooting or catching. In recent years, this has been put as high as £30,000 per stag, £1,000 per brace of grouse, and £13,000 per caught salmon (a recent sale of fishing rights on the River Beauly was assessed on the basis of £12,000 per fish caught annually). This can raise the cost of estate purchase phenomenally, and make it attractive only to wealthy overseas purchasers or institutions, especially since, unlike those in England, Scottish sporting estates are liable for local rates. Estate land values increased by 200 per cent in 5 years in the late 1980s.

An important side effect of the value placed on shootable red deer stags is that it can discourage owners from substantially reducing their deer stocks, even where this is clearly necessary for the health of the land. The deer population, largely as a result of recent mild winters and insufficient culling of the hind population, has now reached record numbers, often preventing the regeneration of native woodlands, and causing serious damage in commercial plantations. It is estimated that an annual cull of 27,000 hinds is required simply to maintain the status quo. (An official agency, the Red Deer Commission, has been established to promote good deer-management practice). The high cost of sporting estates has also put pressure on managers to maximise revenues and to reduce disturbance of game to a minimum, so that there is an increasing tendency to positively discourage public access on some estates despite a long standing tradition of freedom to walk in the Scottish hills.

Apart from the great forestry plantations, sporting estates now occupy by far the largest proportion of the Scottish uplands, still recognised as the most extensive tracts of open semi-natural country in Britain. These open uplands were identified internationally as far back as 1980 in the World Conservation Strategy by the International Union for the Conservation of Nature as a unique "mixed mountain and moorland" ecosystem in need of special protection at the global level.

CHAPTER 9
Lairds and Crofters

Take a journey through Lochaber, Laggan, Badenoch, Glenmore and Strathaven, and when you come to a wild, desert glen, you need not trouble to enquire who is the proprietor. You may take it for granted it is the Duke of Gordon, and you would scarcely refrain from the Englishman's apostrophe to Invercauld, 'D-n that fellow, I believe he hath got the whole highlands.'

James Hogg – *Highland Tours* (1803)

SCOTLAND HAS THE MOST concentrated land ownership in Europe. As Sir John Sinclair stated in his report on the agricultural state of Scotland in 1814:

'In no country in Europe are the rights of proprietors so well defined and so carefully protected.'

Ownership of large areas in Scotland tends to be continuous; throughout the last 9 centuries, less than 1,500 estates have owned the majority of the land. Much of this is the result of the granting

of lands to the original Anglo-Norman families, mainly to extend the authority of the Crown and to raise forces for its defence. To this day, elements of the same feudal system persist in the rights of landowners to control activities (including some forms of development) on land previously owned by them and now under a feu-hold tenure (the feudal system was effectively abolished in England in 1290). Unlike most other European countries, there are no controls on the sale or purchase of any acreage of land in Scotland and without a compulsory land register it is often very difficult to ascertain land ownership, a feature which may make it attractive to some.

Where land is under a tenancy, it is common for the landlord to retain certain rights, for example hunting and shooting, mineral exploitation, access, woodland management and so on. Whereas the number of landowners has increased in the last century, there has not been anything like the same increase in the feudal superiorities, so these still remain very concentrated. The distribution of property rights in Scotland is very much more complicated than the pattern of actual land holdings, due to this hierarchy of superior rights, which are not readily identifiable. (Shetland was one area of Scotland not affected by feudalism and it still has, under the old Norse Udale law, the form of common ground known as 'scattalds'.) Private ownership was considerably extended by a single Act in 1695, which allowed neighbouring landowners to claim the very considerable lands held as 'commonties' from before feudal times for local public usage, whether for grazing, hay cutting or turbary (peat cutting), and this was gradually extended to include previous Crown and Church lands.

Unlike England, there were no early Enclosure Acts, and the process of taking over these commonties was relatively simple. After the failure of the 1745 rising, large areas of clan lands in the Highlands held by clan chiefs who supported Prince Edward Charles Stuart were made forfeit by the Crown and given to those loyal to the Hanoverian cause. The new owners were encouraged to improve the land by enclosure, often carried out under the terms of the new longer leases and tenancies which were granted in the later 18th century. From this time onwards, rent payment was more often in cash rather than in produce and military service. Changing agricultural fortunes, and a rapidly rising population unable to pay the higher rents demanded, led to the infamous Clearances of crofting populations in the late 18th and 19th centuries and the purchase of large areas of land by successful industrial magnates. In the latter half of the 19th century, this led to the establishment of the great shooting estates which are such a feature of Highland land ownership up to the present time.

In the 1870s these great estates comprised nearly 60 per cent of Scotland; although this has reduced, the number of estates of over 400 hectares/1,000 acres has remained more or less constant for a long time. Estates such as these account for 75 per cent of all privately held land, and there is still a progression towards fewer and larger land units, although most of this is on less valuable remote land. There has been a barely perceptible change in the number of estates above 405 hectares/1,000 acres between 1870 and the 1990s - it is possible that 25 per cent of all estates have been held by their respective families for 400 years or more, and the areas of Scotland with historically extensive private ownership in the Borders and Highlands are still the ones with the largest proportion of large scale private ownership today. Ten per cent of the country is actually held by only 13 landowners, the largest of these being the Duke of Buccleuch with approximately 108,000ha/270,000 acres. Another way of expressing this is that 0.001 per cent of the population own 57 per cent of the land. Simultaneously, there has been a marked fall in the total proportion of land held by large estates, largely due to the increase in state-owned land and owner-occupied farms. At present, half the land is held by fewer than 600 estates of 2,000ha/5,000 acres or more and a third of the land is contained within only 120 estates of 8000ha/20,000 acres or more.

An increasing proportion of sporting land has in recent years been sold to purchasers from outside the country and there have also been many sales to large institutions and commercial companies. The estimated capital value of such estates is usually tied to the current value of available game, which can produce wildly inflated paper values for land which is amongst the poorest in Europe. The largest area of publicly owned land is held by the Forestry Commission with approximately 720,000ha/1,800,000 acres, followed by the Department of Agriculture and Fisheries with 178,000ha/445,000 acres. With defence lands totalling about 19,160ha/48,900 acres, the total publicly owned land in Scotland is approximately 8.5 per cent. The National Trust for Scotland owns 76,000ha/190,000 acres – in recent years, conservation bodies have become substantial landowners, managing over 120,000ha/300,000 acres.

Another Way of Life

They had their own ideology, which was that possession of land - the tenure
(not the ownership) of a croft - was the highest good a man could desire.

T C Smout – *A Century of the Scottish People* (1986)

A croft has been somewhat cynically defined as 'a small farm surrounded by regulations' but crofting is much more than agriculture. A crofting 'township' is misleading, since the widely spaced small-holdings represent more a community of common interest than any collection of buildings called a town. Crofting is not a minority interest; there are 17,700 registered crofts within the old 'crofting' counties stretching from Shetland to Argyll, occupying 20 per cent of the Highlands and Islands area. Of these 85 per cent are tenanted, rather than owned, but the crofter now has the option of purchasing his croft, while his tenancy has been well secured by a series of Parliamentary Acts. The Crofting Estates (Scotland) Act came into force in June 1997 allowing crofters on Scottish Office crofting estates to put forward proposals to establish crofting trusts.

These late-19th century Acts were a response to the widespread civil disturbances arising from crofting conditions and the infamous Clearances which had started in the previous century. A combination of population increases from the 1750s onwards, land shortage, and a series of bad harvests contemporaneous with potato blight had made the crofters, in the words of the 20th century Lewis crofter, Frank Rennie, 'hungry, poor, landless, and desperate'. Much of their desperation stemmed from their treatment at the hands of rapacious chiefs and their land factors, which prompted Donald MacAskill at a Land Reform meeting in 1884 to say: 'I am ashamed to confess it now that I trembled more before the factor than I did before the Lord of Lords'. Crofting therefore has a folk history which has developed a powerful community solidarity and feeling for the land, beyond either ownership or farming as such.

Crofts vary enormously in size and situation, but typically may comprise about 2ha/5 acres with access to communal rough grazing (often nowadays improved by fertilising and re-seeding) and a peat bank. On this scale, a croft on its own cannot usually provide a living, although there are still a few full-time crofts. More commonly, one or more members of the family will be in employment locally; however the croft income, albeit small, is often important in retaining the rural population in areas where employment is difficult and may be seasonal. There are still croft houses producing their own tweed, although the Harris tweed industry has declined considerably in recent years, with changes in fashion and the advent of lightweight man-made fibres. On the coast, in-shore fishing, especially for lobsters, can provide a valuable income supplement. Croft land is often distributed in a strip pattern, from the relatively fertile coastal machair (dune meadow) to the inland hill moor, known as 'black land'. There is still a tradition of communal activity for peat cutting or potato planting.

Typically, the unit will support one or more score of sheep, possibly some cattle, and arable ground used for growing fodder crops, including hay, turnips, kale and potatoes. Unfortunately, sheep have largely replaced cattle, whose grazing and trampling are considered to be better for both the land and wildlife; cattle make more demands on time, which may not fit easily with outside employment. It is usually impractical or uneconomic to apply pesticides and other chemicals (apart from limited areas which are improved by fertiliser) so that crofting offers a striking comparison to the intensive farming on large lowland units. The latter are now usually highly specialised in the crops or livestock raised, compared to the traditional mixed farming of the crofting areas which provides such a rich variety of wildlife habitats.

CHAPTER 10

The Progress of Industry

Any examination of what is distinctive about Scotland at this uncertain time in its history comes swiftly to confront the continuing preoccupation of Scots with industrial matters ... industrial decline remains . . . a talisman of national grievance.

Keith Aitken – *Anatomy of Scotland* (1992)

PRIOR TO THE INDUSTRIAL revolution, industry in Scotland was very much tied to local resources, eg the medieval coal mining and salt manufacture around the shores of the Forth, and the production of charcoal for smelting from the remaining extensive coppiced oakwoods in the west. Coal mining was developed in Lanarkshire, Fife and the Lothians from the 15th century. Subsequently, coal was much in demand for the production of lime for spreading on fields to raise productivity. In the late Middle Ages, important exports to northern Europe included salt, hides and, increasingly, wool. Weaving was to remain a home-based cottage industry until the 19th century, and until the mid-19th century most transport was by water; the appalling condition of Scotland's roads up to this time was remarked upon by many travellers.

The opening up of trade with America saw Glasgow develop in the 18th century as an important centre and port for cotton, tobacco, and other commodities. Substantial changes resulted from the emigrations from Ireland and the Highlands to the industrial labour centres, including Dundee with its important linen and later jute industries, latterly founded on Empire trade. The amount of coal mined trebled in the 19th century, but until the Act of 1842 limited the age of employment of children, it was not unusual to see seven year olds going down the pits, where women would grow old before their time carrying 80kg/170 lb of coal on their backs uphill for 8 pence a day. There was a huge development of specialised heavy iron and steel manufacture based on the great mechanical engineering and power inventions of the late 18th and 19th centuries. Scotland became famous as the workshop of the Empire in the building of bridges and ships and for the production of engines and locomotives which were exported world-wide. In 1913, the Clyde alone launched about 750,000 tons of shipping, more than the total output of Germany or the USA and about 18 per cent of world production. Scotland at that time manufactured about one fifth of the UK's steel output and employed 140,000 coal miners.

These industries were supported by a parallel development in transport and communications. The early turnpike and toll roads established in the 18th century were used by the first regular coach services between Edinburgh and London by the 1750s and the much more reliable mail coaches towards the end of that century. Canals such as the Forth and Clyde built from the 1750s onwards were important to service Lowland industrial centres and over 900 properly engineered gravel roads were constructed in less than 20 years by Thomas Telford to open up the Highlands at the beginning of the 19th century. The first public railway (Kilmarnock and Troon) was in service in 1811 and was followed by a rash of railway building throughout the country. In 1812, the first steamboat service in Europe was provided by the 'Comet' between Glasgow and Greenock.

The relatively narrow and interdependent base of the heavy industries made the Scottish economy vulnerable to subsequent competition from overseas, especially from countries with cheap labour, and there was a decline from the end of the 19th century. The boost of World War I was followed by a world recession which was especially severe in Scotland, resulting in massive unemployment in the late 1920s and early 1930s and a continuous reduction in the traditional industries based on coal, iron and steel, which previously employed large numbers. By 1933, the Clyde was launching only 56,000 tons of shipping, and 69 per cent of the workers in that industry were unemployed. The mining workforce was reduced to almost half of what it had been 20 years previously. Average income per head in Scotland dropped from about 92 per cent of the UK average in the late 1920s to 86 per cent by 1933.

The Modern Economy

What is not in doubt is that the Scots will continue to regard economic development as a key measure of the health of their nation.

Keith Aitken – *Anatomy of Scotland* (1992)

Although 237 collieries were still operating in 1947, by the 1980s it was clear that deep mining was becoming increasingly costly, with narrow coal seams and reduced demand, partly because of restrictions on polluting fuels. This decline has continued until the present day with only one deep mine remaining.

Since the 1950s, there has been a radical transformation of the Scottish economy, with the replacement of heavy industries and textiles with light engineering, electronics (including computers), scientific and medical instrumentation, and a major shift towards the service sector, including finance and tourism. From 1954 onwards there was a quantum increase in electronics and scientific instrument manufacture, greatly assisted by inward investment mainly from the USA. About 1 in 20 jobs are directly related to the oil industry, often providing alternative employment for those in declining merchant marine, ship building and fishing sectors. However, the cyclical characteristics of the oil industry, with slumps in oil prices, have made this a volatile economy reflected, for example, in sudden closures of rig construction yards.

Although the immediate post-war development boosted the construction and engineering industries, their share of the market has declined, while food processing, drinks and tobacco manufacture has increased; taken together these comprise the biggest employing sector in Scottish manufacturing, with 70,000 employees. Nevertheless, the proportion of the work force employed in production (as opposed to services) has fallen, as there have been substantial falls in employment in the primary resource-based industries such as agriculture, forestry and fishing, partly due to increased mechanisation. One of the largest drops in employment has been in mining and quarrying (over 70,000) while professional and scientific employment has risen by over 200,000. There have been considerable reductions in employment within transport industries due to the rise in private car ownership.

A significant post-war development has been the establishment of New Towns, built to house more than one quarter of a million people and to encourage new enterprises by special incentives, which have attracted many of the high-tech companies. However, compared to the traditional extractive and manufacturing industries, these capital-intensive activities employ relatively few people. By contrast, it is estimated that tourism now accounts for 8 per cent of all jobs with a value estimated at £2.1 billion or over 5 per cent of the Scottish Gross Domestic Product, ahead of electronics and drinks, although well behind the financial sector which claims 15 per cent. In Highland Scotland tourism is calculated to account for 20 per cent of the economy, generating £500 million per year.

Although the Scottish economy is now very similar structurally to that of the rest of the UK, it has a lower proportion of employment in manufacturing. Despite the rise in the service sector, productivity in Scotland's manufacturing sector is higher than in the UK as a whole, albeit on a vulnerably narrow base.

Energy from Land and Sea

Instead of going out to a byre to see a cow calving with the old paraffin lamp, which is beautifully romantic ... to click on that light and click it off again and go back to your bed is marvellous.

Ben Coutts – *Highland Air* (1990)

In terms of energy, Scotland is quite distinct from the rest of the UK in using indigenous resources of peat, water and oil – although of course oil is used south of the border, the main fields all lie within the Scottish sector of the North Sea, while neither hydropower or peat is used in England. The resources themselves are intimately linked to the climate, geology and geography of the country. In the case of peat, changes in climate some 2,000 years ago combined with deforestation led to the extensive deposits which occur throughout the north of Scotland, formed when the weather became cooler and moister, thus slowing down organic decomposition and soil development. Peat formed elsewhere in former lake basins, the vegetation under the water building up and eventually producing today's raised bogs. The peat can vary from a thin layer on the surface, interspersed by rocky ground which makes it difficult to extract economically, to substantial stretches of deposits several metres deep.

Peat stacks are very much a feature of the northern and western landscapes of Scotland, the geometry of their construction varying from place to place, sometimes according to the taste of the owner. The small piles of peat left at intervals along the margins of the peat banks on the moorland are left there to dry in the wind, before being transported to the back of the croft house and rebuilt, usually with great care and neatness, as the winter store of fuel. Following recent rises in fuel prices, notably oil in the early 1970s, ownership of a peat bank is now much sought after, despite the intensive labour involved in cutting and stacking. It is reckoned that 15,000 to 20,000 peats, each approximately the size of a brick, are required each year to keep a croft household in fuel, with fires often kept going throughout the seasons. An expert peat cutter can cut 1,000 peats a day, not counting the assistance needed to lift and stack the heavy turves.

Unlike Ireland, Scotland has never successfully developed its peat resources as a commercial fuel on any scale, despite several attempts in the post-war years, partly because the deposits are so far from population centres and because of their fragmented distribution. However in recent years, machines capable of cutting and extracting peat from below the surface have been used to develop a

local industry for domestic fuel use, even in places distant from peat resources. Horticultural quality peat, usually cut from the previously extensive raised bogs of central Scotland, is still in demand, although gardeners are being encouraged to use alternatives as a conservation measure. Considerable quantities of peat are also burned in the process of whisky distilling, especially for the darker single malts of Islay, where there are plentiful local supplies of peat. Vast areas of peatland in the north-west have been deep-ploughed for tree planting, although satisfactory growth on this wet acid ground is usually dependent on heavy fertiliser application.

The Ice Age is partly responsible for the development of hydropower in Scotland, since the ice-carved corries of the mountain areas provide the best potential high-level dam sites. The first electricity generated in Scotland by hydropower was at Greenock in 1882, and in 1896 a much more ambitious scheme was completed at Foyers on Loch Ness to serve the British Aluminium smelter. However, it was not in the Highlands, but in Galloway that the first large hydro scheme was developed in 1935, linking a series of lochs. Two-thirds of Scotland, mostly within the Highland area, is served by hydro-electricity, over 50 schemes having been constructed immediately after World War II, ranging from quite small and remote stations to giant pump storage schemes. In 1948, only 5 per cent of farms and crofts in northern Scotland had mains electricity, but by 1975 this had leapt to 91 per cent as a result of the activity of the North of Scotland Hydro Electric Board. There was enormous enthusiasm for the exploitation of Scotland's abundant hydro potential, and over a period of 20 years no less than 84 dams and 56 power stations were constructed. The distribution network covers some 60,000km/ 37000miles, with one stretch over the Corrieyairack Pass between Dalwhinnie and Fort Augustus in Inverness district rising to 764m/2,507ft. By 1960 all the best hydro-power sites had been identified and exploited, but one estimate suggests that there may be a total hydro-electric potential in Scotland of around 2000 megawatts, representing a 70 per cent increase on present capacity. The principal rivers used for hydropower generation are the Tay, Tummel, Beauly, Conon and those flowing into the Great Glen, such as the Garry and the Moriston.

The most northerly scheme is on Loch Shin since the Northern Isles have no significant hill areas and consequently no volume of fast-flowing water. North-east of Inverness, the Conon Valley Scheme has involved 7 linked generating stations and main dams, 32km/20 miles of tunnels and 24km/15 miles of aqueducts. Perhaps the most spectacular scheme is Ben Cruachan on Loch Awe, Argyll. This is one of two pumped storage schemes (the other being at

Foyers on Loch Ness) with water being pumped to a high dam utilising spare overnight generating capacity from thermal stations to
supply the heavier daytime demands. The dam, over 333m/1,000ft.
long and 51m/153ft. high, has been constructed at the edge of a
great ice corrie high on the slopes of the mountain. Here the rainfall averages 3,000mm/120 inches, falling throughout the year to
replenish the dam waters. The machine hall for the turbines,
linked by giant tunnels covering the area of a full-sized football
pitch and high enough to accommodate a seven-storey building,
has been excavated out of the solid granite of Ben Cruachan – not
surprisingly, the whole scheme is now an important tourist attraction.

Hydro-electricity has transformed living and working conditions in the Highlands, but the closure in the 1980s of the aluminium smelter at Invergordon, a major consumer of hydro-electric power, was a severe blow. Although it is a non-polluting form
of generation, there is still considerable impact on the environment, including large dam and power station construction, and
not least, the effects of lines of tall pylons marching across a very
bare landscape (submarine cables provide the principal link to the
main island groups). The draw-down of water levels within the
dammed areas often creates an exposed and barren loch shore,
while diverted rivers can leave unattractive eroded river beds.
Although the electricity authorities have made considerable
efforts, building fish ladders (the well-known one at Pitlochry is a
good example) and passes, fishermen are critical that many of the
schemes have seriously affected runs of salmon and trout where
water has been diverted for power generation. Electricity is also
generated by the two main nuclear stations in Scotland at
Hunterston on the Ayrshire coast and the more recent Torness
near Dunbar on the Forth.

North Sea oil is the latest natural resource to have been
exploited and has not only rejuvenated many parts of Scottish
industry, but has been a mainstay of the U.K economy from the
mid 1970s onwards (although drilling started as early as 1964).
Oil exploitation was not new to Scotland, since the mineral has
been extracted from the West Lothian deposits of oil shale from
the late 1850s – an industry which survived for a further 100
years. At the outset of the exploration and development phase in
the North Sea, there was considerable anxiety about the environ-

mental effects, both on-shore and at sea, from the construction of oil rigs and the development of fabrication yards to the siting of terminals and the threat of oil pollution. Although there have been highly-publicised incidents such as the wrecking of the Braer oil tanker off Shetland in January 1993 (which was quite unrelated to Scottish oil development) many of these fears have proved unfounded, with considerable credit going to the various planning authorities, notably in the Northern Isles, for imposing strict controls on the industry. The extensive pipeline system for both oil and gas running much of the length of Scotland has been constructed with minimal impact on the landscape, so that it is not possible to identify these routes from casual observation. North Sea oil development has stimulated innovative environmental assessment and planning control approaches, and these methods and successes have been examined by may other countries anxious to learn from the Scottish experience.

The economic effects have been more significant, with more than £100 billion in revenues since the first oil came ashore in 1975. There was a huge leap in production from 1.6 million tonnes in that year to 80 million tonnes in 1979. The UK has been a net exporter of oil from 1980 onwards, and is the biggest natural gas extractor in Europe. By 1980, it was estimated that over 46,000 people were employed directly in the industry, the highest proportion (33,000 in 1981) in Grampian Region, although 30 per cent of the off-shore workers came from England. Production peaked at 122 million tonnes in 1985, and following a price slump and declining production was slowly rising again in 1993.

Away from the oilfields, natural geography has often dictated the location of the main developments: sheltered deep water as in the Clyde and Moray Firth for the construction and launching of rigs, or accessible landfalls for pipelines and terminals such as Sullom Voe in Shetland (the largest in Europe covering more than 1,000 acres), Flotta in Orkney and Hound Point in the Firth of Forth. This has also determined the main landfall for natural gas at St Fergus on the north Aberdeenshire coast. Nearly all of these developments have occurred in 'greenfield' sites, rather than the traditional heavy industrial centres, although the shipbuilding and marine engineering skills of these areas have been invaluable to the industry. An important by-product of oil development has been the improvement in support infrastructure, notably communica-

tions, especially air transport; air movements from the small airport at Sumburgh in the Shetlands for example increased from
1,900 in 1969 to 800,000 ten years later, necessitating a considerable expansion of facilities. In the same period, the population in
Aberdeen increased by 30,000 and a comparable number of new
houses were built there, resulting in house price rises of nearly 500
per cent in some sectors.

Windmills have been known in Scotland from medieval times,
but only a few wind turbines for generating electricity have been
installed in Scotland, largely because of the surplus availability of
energy (Scotland being a net exporter) from other sources.
However, Scotland has the best wind-power potential in the whole
of Europe, and commercial generation has started in Orkney from
the turbine on Burgar Hill, which produces more power than any
other windmill in the world due to the islands' strong winds. With
plentiful wind and water resources, Scotland has an unusually
high potential for power generation from these non-polluting
sources, but there is opposition from those who consider that their
visual impact and noise is unacceptable.

The Water of Life

*In so narrow a country ... we cannot expect to find rivers
Danube, but when their rapidity and the shortness of their
courses are kept in view, we must allow that the Scottish
streams are by no means inconsiderable.*

Robert Heron – *Scotland Delineated* (1799)

Uisge beatha (Gaelic for 'water of life') or whisky is only one of
the many industries that benefit from Scotland's plentiful high-
quality water. The statistics for water in Scotland are impressive -
Loch Ness contains more water than all the lakes and reservoirs in
England and Wales combined, while the largest area of fresh water
in Britain is Loch Lomond at 71.1sq km/27sq miles. Loch Morar,
with a maximum depth of 310m/1,000ft, is the deepest freshwater body in Britain and among the 20 deepest freshwater bodies in
the world. The Tay is the longest river in Britain at 193km/

120miles, with the largest catchment and an average flow twice that of the River Thames. Of the 31,000 lochs and lochans, 81 are developed for water supply, supplemented by 238 artificial reservoirs. Many of these reservoirs, for example in the low hill ranges around the central Lowlands are relatively small and, if anything, enhance rather than detract from the environment.

Although Scotland has a reputation for its rainfall, in some east coast areas this drops to about 50cm/20in per annum and some irrigation is now used on the drier coastal farmland. This is compensated for in the west by rainfall which can average 200cm/80in per annum, providing enormous potential for industry and hydro power: about 20 per cent of river and loch catchments in the Highland area have been extensively modified by hydro-electricity schemes. Most of the river systems were established during the Ice Age and there is evidence that southern fish are still prospecting these northern waters where the habitats are suitable. The water systems have been used as routeways from the beginning of known history and the lochs have even been used as defensive settlements; lake dwellings and 'crannogs' can still be identified in Scottish lochs today. Many towns in Scotland owe their present location to their proximity to rivers, for defence and transport, as convenient crossing points and trading centres, and because rivers and burns could be used to power mills.

At the present time, Scotland uses just over one per cent of its available water, and there are serious proposals to supply the surplus commercially to the drier south of England via giant pipelines. Scotland is fortunate in having minimal dependence on underground water supplies, since the surface water from its many lochs and rivers, yielding 3,515 megalitres per day, can meet over 97 per cent of its requirements. It is also particularly favoured in having high quality water, which is crucial not only for such industries as whisky and fish farming, but also to maintain the reputation of its sport fisheries. By the standard chemical classification, only 3.2 per cent of non-tidal rivers and canals in Scotland are considered polluted, although there have been much-publicised cases of 'enrichment' leading to widespread green algal blooms on such famous fishing lochs as Loch Leven in Kinross. As elsewhere, a proportion of this pollution is known to be the result of agricultural practices, including heavy fertiliser application and subsequent field run-off into water systems, and leakages from silos.

Acid rain is implicated in the dramatic decline in fish in some Galloway lochs in granite areas.

Manufacturing industry in Scotland is the highest user of water – the giant petrochemical complex at Grangemouth alone uses three to four million gallons daily from Loch Lomond. Paper-making is also a high user, as was steel manufacture, before the closure of the main production facilities. Hydro-electricity gener-ation uses the greatest volume of water not involved in cooling processes, the latter making up a third of all industrial effluent. Domestic water supply requirements for the population of just over 5 million people (who each use an average of 22 gallons daily) is relatively modest. Edinburgh was one of the first cities in the UK to ensure a continual water supply for a growing popula-tion by the construction of the Glencorse and Loganlea reservoirs in 1821 and 1847 respectively.

Public use is not however confined to domestic purposes, since the lochs and rivers of Scotland are prime recreational and sport areas, not least for fishing. Loch Katrine is a good example of a water body considerably altered for water supply for the expand-ing 19th century population of Glasgow, but which is now an important recreational resource. The 54km/34 mile long submerged aqueduct required the original loch to be raised by 5m/17ft, yet this did not deter the many thousands of visitors who came to the area last century prompted by with its association with Sir Walter Scott's novel, *The Lady of the Lake*. Although the increased sophistication of water treatments has reduced the conflicts between water quali-ty standards for public consumption and recreation, the popularity of some areas close to built-up areas (such as Loch Lomond) has created problems of bank erosion, pollution and disturbance to wildlife and people from power boating, jet-skiing and so on.

Getting from Here to There

Up to Ullapool I had been driving over good and moderately level roads. From now on I was to find myself climbing up and down mountain sides over surfaces little better than cart tracks.

Edwin Muir – *Scottish Journey* (1935)

Had Edwin Muir been journeying 150 years earlier he would have found most of the so-called roads in central and south Scotland 'little better than cart tracks', and until the 19th century it would have been considerably easier to travel to different parts of Scotland by sea rather than land. Two hundred years ago there was no road system for wheeled vehicles north of Inverness and there are still places on the west coast, such as Inverie in Knoydart, which can only be reached by boat. The most important of the Roman roads in Scotland, Dere Street, linking Hadrian's Wall in Northumbria to Edinburgh, was the first road passable by wheeled vehicles. Fords and local ferries were important for river crossings in the absence of bridges. Apart from the Roman roads which were used throughout the medieval period, the earliest roads were probably the drove routes for the driving of large numbers of cattle to market in the south (though 'road' is probably an exaggeration for these rough tracks through the high passes and hills). There is little doubt that poor land communications severely hampered the unification and development of the country until General Wade provided a network of over 1,000 miles of military roads and bridges in the Highlands from the mid 18th century onwards. Despite the fact that these roads were primarily meant for rapid troop movements to keep the Highlands in order following the abortive Jacobite Rising in 1715, the appreciation of their other uses was expressed at the time:

> *"Had you seen these roads before they were made,*
> *You'd lift up your hands and bless General Wade!"*

It was not until 1786 that the first mail coach service between London and Edinburgh was established, about 10 years after the first canal had been built between the Forth and the Clyde, but the subsequent deepening of the Clyde itself was equally important.

The Caledonian Canal, built to avoid the stormy passage round the West Coast of Scotland to Inverness, was completed in 1847 by that notable Borders engineer, Thomas Telford, who was also responsible for constructing more than 1,600km/1,000 miles of road and 1,200 bridges throughout Scotland from 1801 onwards. However, the importance of the Caledonian Canal and others was eclipsed by the arrival of the railways: the first main line between Edinburgh and Glasgow was opened in 1842, but railways did not reach Inverness until 1861. The railways spelled the end of the old coaches, and cattle droving died out as train transport of stock and other agricultural produce was much more efficient. The power of the commercial railways was such that they were permitted to build their stations in the very centre of the cities, including Edinburgh and Glasgow, despite the disruption and pollution involved. The railways certainly encouraged the growth of Scottish towns, and made commuting possible from extended suburbs, even from the Clyde islands, with their improved ferry services.

By 1880 the railway network was almost complete, with dozens of lines crossing the central lowlands. To some extent, the efficiency of these services and their absorption of capital inhibited the improvement in the road system prior to the appearance of the internal combustion engine. It was of course the railway that stimulated the building of the Forth Bridge, at that time the longest single span steel bridge in the world, with its two giant steel arches, each half a kilometre in length.

By 1895, the Euston express had reduced the journey from Aberdeen to London to the phenomenal time of eight and a half hours. However, the railways did not extend to many of the west coast ports, apart from Mallaig, Oban and Kyle of Lochalsh, and until relatively recently the steam 'puffers' operating out of the Clyde provided a lifeline to many of the smaller Highland and island communities. Scotland's railway system was almost halved between 1957 and 1985 from over 3,200 to 1,700 miles, with the abandonment of many rural branch lines, and the loss of some of the most scenic railway routes in Europe. There has been a concentration of investment in the profitable intercity network, and the electrification of the Glasgow to London and Edinburgh to London routes in the 1970s reduced the journey time of the latter to just over four hours.

The steam 'puffers' that served the west coast made good use of the Crinan Canal, built in 1801 to avoid the hazardous journey, then under sail, around the Mull of Kintyre, and subsequently linked to a passenger service from Glasgow. Today it is mainly a route for yachtsmen from their Clyde moorings to the west coast cruising area. The improvement in steamship and ferry services in the 19th century, often linked to connecting rail services, greatly enhanced tourism in the west of Scotland particularly, giving a boost to such towns as Oban and Fort William. Ferry services to the Northern and Western Isles are still important as the main transport for both passengers and heavy goods, with 120 ship and boat services in the Highland area alone. The chief mainland departure ports are Mallaig, Oban and Ullapool, with Uig on Skye linking Tarbert on Harris and Lochmaddy on North Uist, but it is Lerwick in Shetland which now has the greatest weight of traffic passing through any port in Britain, due to oil transport. The survival of all of the island communities is heavily dependent on these services, and proposals to cut the unprofitable routes to the smaller islands have been fiercely resisted. Many ferries are now roll-on, roll-off and carry increasing numbers of tourists who are important to the island economies.

Prior to World War II, private vehicle transport was still a relative luxury for most Scots, with only 1 in 30 owning a car. By 1985 there were 1.25 million private vehicles, or 1 for every 4 people and in 1994 the total number of vehicles registered (including commercial vehicles) was approximately 2 million – a 31 per cent increase over the decade. By 1995 some 50-60 per cent of all journeys to work were by private transport. In the same year, there were over 200 miles of motorway in use, mostly within the Central Belt, and the journey time from Edinburgh to Inverness has been reduced from almost a whole day expedition, even as late as the 1960s, to a few hours. Notorious Highland roads, such as the feared Devil's Elbow which required pre-war cars to go into reverse, have been straightened and widened, while others, such as the road across Rannoch Moor, have been abandoned in favour of new routes, although there are still many single-track roads with passing places in the central and north-west Highlands. There is often a difference of view between local residents who not unnaturally are enthusiastic about improved roads, and tourists for whom the single-track roads convey a pleasing sense of another era and an excuse to slow down.

The last 30 years have seen the building of important new bridges across the Forth, Tay, Clyde and Cromarty Firths - an indication of the increase in vehicle use is shown by the 60 per cent rise in the number of vehicles using the main toll bridges between 1984 and 1995, while many by-passes and ring roads now circumnavigate town centres such as Edinburgh, Glasgow, Aberdeen, Dundee and Stirling. Urban motorways, such as that in Glasgow, involved the destruction of over 700 houses and divided and isolated whole communities. Previously, inner-city transport was provided in all the main cities of Scotland by tramway, but these had largely vanished by the late 1950s, although those in Glasgow survived until 1962. Their place was taken initially by buses, but increasingly by private vehicles which are now creating very serious problems of congestion and pollution, especially in Edinburgh. Glasgow has reduced its problem by re-establishing its city underground train system. In rural areas, the decline of public transport services, both rail and bus, has stimulated car ownership, but has seriously disadvantaged those without private transport. With the de-regulation of bus services, there are more independent operators concentrating on the most profitable intercity routes - passenger journeys on local buses fell by 16 per cent in the 5 years up to 1995.

Cycling in both town and country is again becoming more popular, but the slow and incomplete development to date of dedicated cycle routes in towns has discouraged an older generation from "getting on their bikes". Nevertheless, increasing incentives are being provided, such as payment of mileage for public servants using pedal power. Mountain biking, which has escalated in recent years, is less a means of communication than a form of recreation, not always welcomed by other countryside users. It is interesting to note how many such bikers use private vehicles to transport their cycles to suitable locations, which may also reflect on the unpleasantness and hazard of cycling on congested roads out of the major towns. Notwithstanding the increasing use of private transport, there is still in Scotland a relatively high proportion of people who either walk to work or use public transport.

Civil aviation reached Scotland in the 1930s with the first service by Highland Airways from Inverness to Orkney in 1933, followed by the development of other routes which were to prove very beneficial to remote communities, not least for hospital and emergency services. The journey by plane from Wick to Kirkwall now took 35 minutes, as opposed to 6 hours by road and boat. World War II stimulated airport construction and air services, with the development of four major airports at Prestwick near Ayr, Renfrew near Glasgow, Turnhouse on the outskirts of Edinburgh, and Dyce near Aberdeen. The latter became the fastest-growing airport in the UK the 1980s due to the oil boom which also made it into the busiest heliport in the world. The Renfrew airport has now been displaced by Abbotsinch, which has also taken all the transatlantic passenger services from Prestwick, and as the busiest airport in Scotland handles almost three million passengers each year. Shuttle services now operate from all the main Scottish airports to London and other cities in the UK. Scotland is distinguished as the only country in Europe, if not in the world, to use a natural beach – on Barra in the Outer Hebrides – as a regular commercial landing "strip" and where the pilot has to be familiar with the tide timetable!

CHAPTER 11

Living Together

A *desert wi' windaes*

Billy Connolly

With over 75 per cent of its total population located in the central Lowlands and some parts of the country with fewer than 10 inhabitants per square mile, Scotland has the most uneven population distribution of any country in Europe. It was not always so, and we know that as late as the mid 18th century, almost half the population could be found north of the Highland line. The evidence from the density of Neolithic hut circles in north-east Perthshire indicates that in Stone Age times there was a higher population in some of the Scottish uplands at relatively high altitude than at any time since, probably under a more clement climate. Later settlements were associated with the Iron Age forts which can be identified on many Scottish hill tops, including Dun Edin (Edinburgh). The subsequent Viking settlements can readily be plotted by the distinctive Norse names for so many of the settlements around the coast of Caithness for instance. Most of these early settlements were in good defensive positions – often overlooking the sea as in the case of the Iron Age brochs on important communication routes.

The first identifiable townships often formed around the castles of early medieval times, and some of these were granted burgh status in the 12th century by King David and his successors. With monopoly on trade, and controlling access via town wall, these feudal settlements became the focal points of whole districts, attracting goods and specialised services alongside the monastic centres which were also granted charters. Good examples of early Royal Burghs are Perth, Dundee and Stirling. The latter demonstrates particularly well the layout of such a burgh with its main street leading to the castle and wynds and pends leading off – a layout which exists in many Scottish towns to this day. Most of these feudal towns are to be found in the Lowlands or in the Border country, such as Dumfries, at an important crossing point, and Old Aberdeen, an ecclesiastical burgh. On the east coast, important market burghs such as Crail established their status through European trade. The powerful burghs with their commercial monopolies almost certainly inhibited the development of villages as such over most of the Scottish countryside.

Most of the settlements in Scotland appear to have changed little until the 18th and early 19th centuries, when there was considerable planning and development of villages and small townships, in some cases establishing quite new and comprehensively planned communities for agricultural services, trade or industry. Huntly in Aberdeenshire, for example was expanded from a very modest local market to accommodate the linen trade; Crieff was replanned as a centre for weaving; while during the latter part of the 19th century the fishing boom stimulated the deliberate layout of Tobermory and Ullapool as fishing townships. Many factory villages were established during this period of the Industrial Revolution, one of the best known being the pioneering social experiment of New Lanark in the middle Clyde valley, where the new owner Robert Owen in the early 19th century, following in the footsteps of his predecessor David Dale, developed an international reputation for his endeavours to create an ideal industrial community, with enlightened views on the welfare of its workers and their dependants.

Many of these villages and townships were deliberately planned and constructed within a relatively short period of time at the instigation of (and often financed by) large landowners, such as the Duke of Gordon in north-east Scotland, where the greatest concentrations of such new settlements are to be found. In the later 19th century, the transformation of communications led to towns like Inverness, at key railheads and interchanges, becoming important regional centres, while railway villages such as Crianlarich owe their existence to this new mode of transport. Around the turn of the century, Mallaig and Kyle of Lochalsh became established steamer ports linked to rail connections. The improvement in communications around towns generally led to suburban residential development as dormitories, often at a considerable distance from workplaces. This has continued to the present time with private transport enabling commuters to live in rural villages while working in the larger centres, as the daily traffic jams leading into Edinburgh from across the Forth Road Bridge testify.

There were considerable population increases in the 18th and 19th centuries: the population of Glasgow tripled from 1841 to 1911, and there were comparable increases in other Scottish cities. Much of this was due to the drift from the land; the population of the crofting parishes fell by around 30 per cent in the 50 years between 1881 and 1931. Significantly, the decrease in the number of children was 41 per cent, while the proportion of people over 61 actually increased by 36 per cent, clear indicators that the remoter rural areas held little prospect for the new generation. However, in lowland areas another important factor was agricultural improvements: while it took 22 man-days to maintain an acre of barley in 1840, this had dropped to 3 man-days by 1958. Overall male employment in agriculture in Scotland dropped from 30 per cent of the total workforce in 1851 to 10 per cent in 1951. Only two-thirds of the number of farm workers in 1951 were employed in agriculture in 1980. An important consequence of this reduction in the rural population has been the decline in local services such as schools, public transport, and shops. However, in the 10 years to 1991, the rural population actually rose by 3.2 per cent while the total Scottish population fell by 1.4 per cent over the same period. This increase tends to be in the older age groups, although there is also some increase in the 25-35 year age range. The present grouping of Scotland's population between cities, towns and villages is interesting because of the relative importance of small settlements, with 45 per cent of the population living in settlements of less than 25,000 or outside settlements altogether.

The steady drift to the towns further concentrated the urban populations, often in desperately overcrowded and unsanitary conditions. Until World War I there was no public housing, and 90 per cent of accommodation was rented privately. In 1917 there were more than four persons per room in over 10 per cent of Glasgow homes, and even as late as 1951 over 15 per cent of Scots were still living in overcrowded conditions with more than two to a room, often without hot water or bath. (at this time the rented tenement flat I lived in boasted a single cold water tap) However, by then 55 per cent of homes were publicly owned, only 10 per cent were rented, and the proportion privately owned had risen dramatically to 35 per cent. In 1990, of just over two million dwellings in Scotland, almost half were owned by public authorities, although many had fallen below tolerable modern standards.

This huge building programme was due partly to the determination of these authorities, both before and after World War II, to clear the inner-city slums such as the Gorbals (which housed 26,000 people) and provide better living conditions.

Many housing estates were built cheaply on the available land not designated as 'green belt' on the margin of cities in the 1950s, but became known for their lack of social and other amenities. Land shortage stimulated the subsequent construction of high-rise blocks, with bleak towers reaching 20 storeys, which prompted Billy Connolly's remark quoted above (there has been a significant movement back into city centre residences, often to the existing tenements many of which have been attractively modernised). These initiatives failed to meet the demand for new houses or employment needs, and to relieve overcrowding and to attract industry and employment, a series of five completely new towns spread across central Scotland were established. The first was founded on the nucleus of the village of East Kilbride near Glasgow in the late 1940s, followed by Cumbernauld, Glenrothes, Irvine and Livingston. Learning from the mistakes of the past, the New Town Corporations designed these New Towns on the concept of self-sustaining 'neighbourhoods' with adequate nearby green space. In terms of inward investment and employment, these New Towns have been a success story - one Scot in 20, about a quarter of a million people, live in these successors to the planned villages of the 18th century, with a total of over 60 per cent home ownership. Despite their undoubted economic success (attracting 11,000 new jobs in 1992), with most of the new electronic industries in Scotland, for example, being located within their boundaries, the New Town Development Corporations are scheduled to be wound up by the end of the century.

CHAPTER 12

Taking the High Road

None but these monstrous creatures of God know how to join so much beauty with so much horror . . . this is so sweetly contrasted with that perfection of nastiness and total want of accommodation that only Scotland can supply.

Thomas Gray – *letter to William Mason*, 12 November 1765

THIS IS HARDLY THE stuff of modern tourist brochures but it reflects the attitudes of the time towards the natural landscapes of Scotland. The very re-moteness of the country to a European is shown in Voitaire's response to Boswell, Dr Johnson's biographer, before these two embarked on their famous tour of the Hebrides:

'He looked at me as if I was going to the North Pole, and said: "You do not insist on me accompanying you?"
"No, sir"
"Then I am very willing you should go!"'

SCOTCHING SOME MYTHS

#1 Of Tartans and Kilts

The assumption that specific tartans denote clan and family in Scotland, is for obvious reasons, promoted by the dresswear industry, but is not supported by the historical evidence. The original 'tartans' would have been irregularly striped or of some form of simple check - sometimes the word was used to denote the fabric itself. There is no indication of tartan as we know it before the 16th century, and it was not until the late 17th century that it appears to have become, albeit loosely, associated with particular families or districts, and certainly there can be no automatic link between surname and tartan pattern. Most tartans worn today are relatively modern and are being continuously created at the request of organisations. Likewise the modern 'little kilt' is very much a cut-down version of the earlier voluminous length of cloth used as a combination of thigh-covering and plaid. A visitor is more likely to encounter the kilt in the Lowlands than in the Highlands, particularly on Saturdays where in recent years, it has become de rigeur for any respectable Scots wedding, with a tartan chosen for style rather than family association. Its present popularity contrasts with its prohibition by Act of Parliament in the post-Culloden years along with other symbols of Gaelic culture and custom.

Until the mid 18th century, travellers' tales from Scotland conveyed an image of a wild, terrifying place, at a time when wilderness was not considered attractive, when access was difficult, the food, accommodation and manners of the people uncivilised, and a visit was fraught with not a little danger. It took the writings and paintings of authors and artists to change the perception of this rough countryside, pre-eminently Sir Walter Scott. It was he who in his fanciful novels created a romantic and mystical image of Scotland, weaving tales that combined the elements of adventurous history against the background of 'mountain and flood', and left in Europe a permanent impression of Scotland which bore little relation to reality. Queen Victoria herself might have been a tourist board copywriter in her eulogies on the Highlands. The combination was potent; the crowds descended on Sir Walter Scott's Trossachs anxious to see the location of *The Lady of the Lake* and *Rob Roy*, and Royal Deeside attracted the curious to Balmoral.

#2 John Knox and All That

The name Knox has somehow become synonomous with extreme and dour Presbyterianism, and a joylessness inevitably associated with "Calvinism" and the renunciation of all earthly pleasures. Above all, Knox's The First Blast Against the Monstrous Regiment of Women earned him the reputation of being a woman-hater in general, although his tract was specifically aimed at Mary Tudor in her position as Queen of England, and to a lesser extent Mary of Guise ruling Scotland as regent at that time. Not only did Knox enjoy the company of women, he married twice, firstly to an Englishwoman, and on the second occasion taking a bride of 16 when he was 59! Contrary to other factions in Scotland, he looked not to Catholic France but to reforming England as an ally in his efforts to secure Protestantism in Scotland, and sent his children to be educated in England. Far from being a strict Sabbatarian and killjoy, he considered Sunday as a good day for a dinner party, enjoyed music, attended the theatre, and even permittted taverns to be opened on a Sunday outwith church service hours. Much of the narrowness of outlook ascribed to Knox can be attributed to his Covenanting successors, forged in the religious strife of the following century.

"When will you Go?" is the Scottish Tourist Board's most recent slogan to maintain an industry in Scotland worth £2.1 billion (5 per cent of the economy) or £350 per head of population, rising to £1,500 in the Highlands and Islands. The yearly number of visitors is twice the total population of Scotland, with 3.5 million travelling to the Highlands alone. English visitors in 1996 spent £973 million, representing an increase over the previous year of 18 per cent – the proportion of domestic to overseas visitors is about 9:1. Scottish tourism employs 177,000 or one full-time job in every 12, but there are many more that are supported by the industry, and a large number of part-time jobs. On the other hand, this work is often highly seasonal – the season may be a short as three months – and although it is often crucial to the economies of the

remoter rural communities, tourism can distort prices and availability of services, and create congestion and environmental problems.

Although it is now the single biggest industry in Scotland there are few purpose-built resorts of any size, much of the activity being centred in small rural and coastal townships. Not surprisingly, a recent survey found that 82 per cent of all visitors place scenery top of their list of attractions: active countryside recreation is estimated to generate £1,000 million and golf, sailing, mountaineering and especially hillwalking are very popular among residents and visitor alike. Overseas visitors favour sites with historic and cultural associations; single historic attractions such as Edinburgh Castle

#3 Money and Meanness

The reputation that Scots have for being tight-fisted - or as they would have it, thrifty - is legendary, to the extent that in Germany, "Schottenpreis" or "Scottish price" indicates a real bargain. Thomas Pennant in 1769 noted that in Aberdeen (where else?)

'The east and west churches are under the same roof; for the North Britons observe economy even in their religion....'

Frugality was raised to a high virtue and its opposite was decried, reflected in Burns *Cottar's Saturday Night*:

And O may Heaven their simple lives prevent
From Luxury's contagion, weak and vile!

The fact that Scots themselves promote this image, not least in telling endless "Aberdonian" jokes against themselves raises a suspicion that their penchant for irony gets in the way of truth. Travellers in earlier times, especially in the Highlands, commented on the almost embarasssing hospitality received at the hands of rich and poor alike, whatever their circumstances, while statistics for donations to charity indicate a higher level of giving from the Scots than elsewhere in UK, with Aberdonians being among the more generous! But perhaps Harry Lauder understood the inverted humour and self-denigration of his countrymen in playing up the sterotype in his remark:

"If folk think I'm mean, they'll no expect too much"

have around a million visitors in any one year. Some 34 per cent of all visitors rate wildlife highly: wildlife sites attract 3.5 million visitors and have an estimated potential to generate £11 million per annum and provide around 1,500 full-time job equivalents. The animals which visitors most want to see are seals, seabirds, birds of prey, sea mammals such as cetaceans, red deer and otters. It is this combination which makes tourism in Scotland distinctive, conveying a very powerful image of dramatic landscapes, observable wildlife, a unique history, a clean open-air country – so much so that the Scottish Tourist Board has been accused of "below the belt" promotion with its advertisements on the London Underground explicitly comparing the breathability of Scotland's air with the congestion of the UK capital.

Of the 35 million day trips made by Scots each year, a high number will involve recreational walking, which is proportionately more popular in Scotland than south of the border, despite the fact that there are relatively few legal rights of way – a fraction of those in England, for example. How-ever, the public freedom to roam the hills is of long standing and jealously guarded by walking and amenity associations. Although the laws of trespass, despite popular belief, are little different from elsewhere in UK, there is a particular tradition in Scotland for landowners to respect the need for the mainly urban population to have access to open country. Changing ownerships have recently resulted in conflicts

#4 Wi a Hundred Pipers

The massed formations of pipers and drummers in their "glitterin gear" assembled for military occasions or festivities is taken to be thoroughly representative of the pageantry of Scotland, yet like their dress and accoutrements, such a spectacle is relatively modern. Bagpipes themselves are by no means the oldest musical instruments played in Scotland, being preceded by the small triangular harp or clarsach known from its depiction on 8th century carved stones. It was the harp which was the favoured pre-battle instrument before the 15th century, while even further back in Pictish times, the bronze war horn or carnyx was used to intimidate the enemy. However, the pipes are of considerable antiquity, with some evidence that they arrived with the Roman legions, possibly via Egypt, but it is not until the 12th century that we have evidence, again from carved stones, of the characteristic wind-bag, since there are several variations on the instrument. Pipes are by no means exclusively Scottish, being found throughout Europe, the Middle East and India and were used regularly in England until at least the 18th century. Today's pipe bands with their formal configurations and quasi-military style derived largely from 19th century regimental developments (often with highly individual embellishments of dress) are a far cry from the individual musicians who were accorded considerable respect as pipers to the chiefs of earlier times, carrying on the traditions of the clan and celebrating its history and achievements in music and dance.

over access, especially on sporting estates anxious to restrict visitors who may disturb stalking or shooting. Some of these estates have been responsible for driving hill roads into remote areas for sporting access, to the detriment of the wilderness experience of public visitors, and the more poorly landscaped roads are undoubtedly eyesores and causes of erosion in mountain areas. It is also true that the ever increasing number of walkers, climbers and skiers not only have the potential to create disturbance, but have caused considerable incidental damage to vegetation and pathways.

#5 Food for horses in England and men in Scotland

Such was the mild dismissal of oats in the time of Dr. Johnson's 18th century travels in Scotland, when this cereal was still the most important staple in the diet of Scots of all classes, intended to reflect the inferior development of the country. Oats became a main crop by about the 6th century, while its anti-oxidant properties were used to preserve other perishable foodstuffs, including meats. Eaten in a variety of forms, it could be easily and quickly prepared as well as being portable, favoured by travellers for its nutritious qualities. (Even recent advertisements suggest it is a necessary prelude to such everyday activities as hammer-throwing and caber-tossing). Yet if Dr. Johnson were to return today, he might be surprised to find that oats in the form of porridge has largely been supplanted by other uncooked cereals at the domestic breakfast table, and is not now always offered in hotels and other boarding establishments, although oatcakes have retained their popularity. It is still an important constituent of that other mysterious symbol of Scottish cuisine, the haggis, which provides, even in its newest vegetarian form, another source of tourist speculation regarding its ingredients. Natives are not slow to hint that it belongs to our natural game species as the justification for being preceded (after its death throes) by proud pipers and laudatory speeches at Burns Suppers.

Generally the impact of tourist activities on the Scottish countryside is localised, even though it can be quite severe where it does occur. Footpath erosion has already been mentioned, as has loch shore erosion caused by the wave action of speed boats and water skiers in popular areas such as Loch Lomond. There have been several protracted battles over the development of downhill skiing facilities in the fragile environment of the Cairngorms, for example, and both boating and fishing have been implicated in disturbance to water bird life. Many caravan sites have been insensitively located and the caravans themselves are certainly a source of irritation on narrow Highland roads, while noisy activities such as jet skiing substantially reduce amenity in otherwise peaceful loch environments. Compared to other parts of the UK however, the pressure of visitors is light and the effects of their activities are by no means widespread, being concentrated in a few popular tourist areas. The commonest epithet applied to Scotland is still "unspoiled" which is perhaps not surprising when over 97 per cent of the land is officially designated as "countryside".

Nevertheless, Scotland has to decide in this matter where its best interests lie. Relative remoteness, costs, and unreliable weather mean that it cannot hope to compete in the mass market with for example, Mediterranean resorts. Increasingly, British residents are taking their main holidays abroad, but are also more frequently indulging in short breaks outwith the main summer season. Scotland is particularly well-placed in being able to offer a wide variety of outdoor activities in incomparable countryside and has successfully marketed these. There seems little doubt that Scotland is regarded as a "quality destination" with the particular attractions of fine landscape, wildlife, history and a distinctive culture. It is unfortunately true that, with notable exceptions, what visitors often encounter is tired tartanry, ersatz mythology, and a low quality of presentation in everything from food to "tradition". At present, apart from an accommodation grading system which is not itself especially clear, there is no obvious way for a visitor to identify quality tourist services despite the "Best of Scotland" and other 'kitemarking' systems.

There are however signs that tourist authorities are beginning to recognise that the upgrading of accommodation facilities in recent years needs to be balanced by an improvement in environmental services and outdoor facilities: it is particularly unfortunate that for example, ranger services have been cut back alongside the previous momentum for improving public access to countryside. More encouraging is the welcome given to a recent trial environmental accreditation scheme for the tourist industry which will be introduced from late 1997.

"When are we going to see a trossach?"
Query by US visitor to the author en route to Loch Lomond

CHAPTER 13

Conserving A Countryside

Just as the conservation of natural resources, perhaps at the last moment, has become a matter of acute concern on a world-wide scale, so we in Scotland begin to know and value what we have been, what we are, and what we might have become.

George Bruce: *from The Future of Scotland, ed. R. Underwood* (1977)

TO KEEP THE COUNTRY 'unspoiled', there is a bewildering number of different forms of protection over the land and almost as many bodies to do the protecting. As elsewhere in the UK however, there is very little of the country that has not been modified to some extent by human activity, often over very considerable periods of time. The remotest islands have supported grazing animals and now even the high tops are being altered by recreation seekers. The earliest conservationists were probably the kings and their nobles anxious to protect their game and hunting quarry by passing

laws to conserve forests, and we do know, for example, of early medieval legislation to protect salmon. The very first bird protection Acts were passed in the 16th century to forbid the spring cutting of grass to feed the town cattle around wildfowl breeding areas on the Boroughmuir, then on outskirts of in

Edinburgh. Protection was almost always to conserve a resource for human use, and it was not until the L9th and 20th centuries that the notion of protecting nature for its own sake arose seriously, although the 18th century landed estates in Scotland led the way in re-creating wooded landscapes around the great houses of the day, mainly for sport and estate enhancement. Many of the first nature reserves established in Scotland owe their existence to the survival of these estates into this century.

Since the end of World War II, most of the main conservation issues that have arisen are similar to those which have caused concern elsewhere in the UK, notably the loss of wildlife habitat due to intensive mechanised agriculture in the Lowlands, industrial development and pollution of estuaries, and the congestion and damage to the urban environment by increased traffic. However, there are several environmental problems that have a particular relevance to Scotland, especially given its image of unspoilt open countryside. Undoubtedly the biggest single change in its famed hill country has been the large scale replacement of sheep farms by commercial conifer plantations, with a considerable impact on the ecology of mountains and moorlands, including the loss of much heather ground and a reduction in numbers of birds of prey. These birds continue to be persecuted by poisoning, shooting and trapping on some of the larger sporting estates in defiance of the law. In 1996 there were no less than 273 reports of such persecution, 141 of these involving birds of prey. The species killed, most by poisoning, included the white-tailed sea eagle, golden eagle, some 24 buzzards and 3 peregrines. On a more optimistic note, the recently reintroduced red kite reared 38 young in 1996.

Overgrazing by both sheep and deer continues, so that natural regeneration of native woodlands is severely restricted, and heather moor is gradually converted to grassland. The hill land is also affected by the increasing number of public visitors, with clear evidence of erosion of footpaths on the most popular routes. Mainly because of its location in the unique environments of the west coast sea lochs, fish farming has aroused concerns, both from the viewpoint of amenity and potential pollution. The prospect of oil development in the Minch raises fears for that rich marine environment, while the most recent threat to the same coast is the proposed development of giant superquarries in localities that offer little other employment. In the Central Belt applications for large

open caste coal mining have stimulated considerable local contro-
versies. Most of these issues concern livelihoods and employment,
however short-term, often in areas where jobs are at a premium -
a concern which lies at the heart of most conservation conflicts in
Scotland.

The UK Protection of Birds Acts in the 19th century enabled a
number of official bird sanctuaries to be established in Scotland and
a number of other nature reserves were given protection by private
owners. One of the most important influences was a philanthropic
Englishman, Percy Unna, who from the late 1930s onwards pur-
chased tracts of mountain country for conservation, including
Glencoe and Kintail, through funds raised by the Scottish
Mountaineering Club (of which he was President) and his own substantial donations. These famous properties were donated to the
National Trust for Scotland, which was subsequently able to acquire
other hill land with the fund established by Unna. Equally importantly, he laid down rules for the management of this open country,
which were to be-come guiding principles for conservationists. Sir
Frank Fraser Darling was another Scottish conservationist who pioneered new thinking on natural resource management through his
writings in the 1930s and 1940s, and which attracted internation-

---

PERCY UNNA
1878–1950

Percy Unna is responsible, almost single-handed, for the conservation of many of
Scotland's finest mountain landscapes. An ardent mountaineer and President of
the Scottish Mountaineering Club in the mid 1930s, he gave very substantial
anonymous donations to the National Trust for Scotland for the purchase of
upland properties, (notably in Glencoe, Kintail and Ben Lawers)) with bequests
which still provide an income for land purchase and management. Unna is now
known especially for 'Unna's Rules' - a set of guidelines which he laid down for
the protection and use of such remote areas. Perhaps anticipating the future popularity of hill walking and other active countryside recreation, together with the
Scottish Mountaineering Club, he stated that these properties should not be
developed, shooting should not be allowed, and that special facilities for public
access, including the creation of new paths, should be avoided. Although in some
quarters, these strictures have been criticised for being out of touch with the
reality of modern recreational demands, and even on National Trust Properties
have not always been followed, there is increasing recognition of Unna's fore-
sight and convictions on the long term needs for conservation of Scottish mountain areas.

al attention before they were recognised here. His early experiences as a naturalist in the remoter parts of Scotland became the foundation for his surveys of National Parks across the globe.

It is difficult to calculate the proportion of Scotland at present designated for some form of conservation since so many of the different forms of protection are overlapping. However, at a conservative estimate it is unlikely to be less than 20 per cent, and in the Highlands and Islands could be significantly more than that. Under the National Parks and Access to the Countryside Act, the Nature Conservancy established the first National Nature Reserve over Beinn Eighe in 1951 covering 4,700ha/11,600 acres of mountain and native pinewood in Wester Ross. Since then, a further 67 National Nature Reserves have been created, ranging from the largest in Europe, the Cairngorms, extending to 26,000ha/64,000 acres of subarctic wilderness to a small juniper wood near Dumfries covering a mere 5ha/12 acres. The total area of such government administered reserves is approximately 112,000ha/280,000 acres, mostly managed by agreement with private owners rather than state-owned, mainly in the mountain areas of the north and west.

Under the Wildlife and Countryside Act of 1981, the areas notified as Sites of Special Scientific Interest have been given protection equivalent to National Nature Reserves covering a similar

---

SIR FRANK FRASER DARLING
1903-79

A naturalist and author, Sir Frank Fraser Darling is perhaps best known to the public through a series of books published in the 1940s including, Island Years and Natural History in the Highlands and Islands. His early work was on the genetics of sheep, but he became attracted to animal behaviour and ecology, notably red deer and colonial birds. His decision to live and work in remote parts of the Highlands enabled him to make direct observations on the relationships between natural history, land use, and man's impact on the Highland environment. A world traveller and international conservationist, he became known in his later years as a passionate advocate for the rights of natural species threatened by modern developments, much of this based on surveys in the US National Parks and in Africa. A prophet before his time, his trenchant comments on the destruction of natural systems and the action needed to correct this were not always well received, either in Scotland or elsewhere, but his originality and perception were recognised in his appointment as vice-president of the Conservation Foundation in the USA and his eventual knighthood. His Reith Lectures in 1969 and their publication in Wilderness and Plenty in 1970 brought him a much wider public recognition as a leading environmentalist of the 20th century.

range in ecological interest and size: at 890,432 ha/2,226,080 acres these now cover over 11 per cent of the land area of Scotland. These are areas of particular value for their flora and fauna, representing all the ecological conditions found in Scotland from the mountains to the coast. A substantial proportion are of geological interest, including for example, Arthur's Seat in Edinburgh. As with National Nature Reserves, these sites are usually privately owned, in some cases with management agreements negotiated with the main Government countryside conservation agency, Scottish Natural Heritage. Such sites are usually held in private ownership, and despite the legislation, are not entirely immune from loss or damage; for example it is estimated that 36 such sites have been seriously degraded by burning, and 25 more damaged by vehicles.

A number of the sites are recognised as being of international importance, such as St Kilda, a World Heritage Site. By 1997, 66 sites had been designated as Special Protection Areas under the European Birds Directive and a further 94 had been registered as Special Areas for Conservation under the European Habitats Directive. Scottish Natural Heritage has recently embarked on an ambitious Species Action Plan covering some 23 vulnerable species from natterjack toads to wood ants and the yellow marsh saxifrage.

There are several forms of protection for important landscapes, mainly by stricter planning controls through the local authorities, such as Areas of Great Landscape Value, of which there are 178, or the much larger area, mainly in upland country, covered by National Scenic Areas: 40 of these cover approximately 13 per cent of the land area of Scotland, within which may also be found many reserves and sites of the kind mentioned above. The general consensus is that such areas do not provide enough protection and fall far short of National Parks, for instance. Much more recent are Environmentally Sensitive Areas which provide conservation management for those owners and farmers prepared to carry out beneficial works, such as replacing dry stane dykes or modifying grazing regimes to favour flora. Covering over 220,000ha/550,000 acres from the Outer Hebrides to the Borders, these have proved popular with farmers in times of agricultural recession.

Many reserves and other areas are managed by voluntary

organisations, the largest being the National Trust for Scotland, with 240,000 members. Although it has important countryside properties, it is best known for its trusteeship of historic buildings and gardens; for example Culzean Castle and Country Park near Ayr has 386,000 visitors each year. By contrast, the Scottish Wildlife Trust is exclusively concerned with wildlife conservation in both town and country, managing almost 90 reserves totalling 18,000ha/44,478 acres. The Royal Society for the Protection of Birds has similar aims, with a particular emphasis on ornithological conservation, and is noted for its successful protection of the osprey on its return to Scotland. Scottish Conservation Projects organises practical conservation work, largely undertaken by volunteers, and related training and education. Such voluntary bodies for the conservation of wildlife are generally more numerous and more effective than their counterparts in the fields of archaeology and protection of the built environment, with the notable exception of the National Trust for Scotland, perhaps a measure of the relatively high profile achieved by nature conservation generally in the UK.

CHAPTER 14

Scotland in Transition

Scotland's a sense of change, an endless becoming for which there was never a kind of wholeness or ultimate category. Scotland's an attitude of mind.

Maurice Lindsay – *Speaking of Scotland, Collected Poems* (1940-90)

The changes in the countryside and the industrial landscape of Scotland have been quite marked over the last 40 years. In the immediate post-war years, there was new investment in machinery and technology, and forestry interests embarked on new plantings on a large scale. In 1950, industry was still largely confined to the Central Belt, and domestic housing was still mainly in established urban settlements. Car ownership was not widespread and railways were still important both for passengers and freight. For those who could afford it, the traditional annual two week holiday in the country or a coastal resort was the norm. In the lowland countryside, many of the old farm steadings are now dominated by massive steel and concrete buildings, many of the hedgerows have gone, and dry stone walls have often been replaced by fences. Sheaves, stooks and threshing machines have been replaced by combine harvesters and grain dryers, all of which have drastically reduced farm labour and eliminated horsepower. Hay crops have given way to silage, and barley is grown year after year on the same ground by massive fertiliser applications. Pigs are re-appearing in open fields and free-range poultry are now more in evidence. Many rural properties are occupied by commuters, and the country dweller without a car is at a severe disadvantage with the decline of rural public transport. Relatively higher fuel prices have further disadvantaged those living in the remoter areas.

In the hills, many of the lower slopes have been reclaimed for cultivation, but the big change has been the expansion of conifer forestry over what was previously sheep ground or heather grouse moor, with a proliferation of hill roads for both forestry vehicles and public access – over half a million hectares have been planted by the Forestry Commission alone in the last 30 years. The mountain areas have also become the focus of recreational development, including winter sports at Cairngorm, Glenshee, Ben Nevis and elsewhere. Mountaineering and hillwalking, previously minority activities, have become increasingly popular, while pony-trekking and mountainbiking are relatively new phenomena. Traditional sport shooting of deer and grouse has declined to an extent, but is still important locally. The relatively modest hydropower development of pre-war years has been overtaken by newer and much larger schemes throughout the Highlands, utilising all the best potential dam sites, and spawning substantial power lines through the countryside.

Scotland is still one of the most highly industrialised countries in Europe, but there have been massive changes in the last 40 years in the pattern and structure of industry. The decline of the heavy industries, especially coal mining, has left its own legacy in derelict industrial landscapes, while new ones, such as the great petrochemical complex at Grangemouth on the Forth and the nuclear power stations of Hunterston in Ayrshire and Torness in East Lothian, symbolise late 20th century Scotland. Many of these developments have been concentrated on the river estuaries, and in the industrial heartland of the Clyde there has been a movement downstream of container-handling facilities to Port Glasgow and Greenock. The changeover from heavy to light industries has stimulated new settlement patterns, especially in the creation of New

Towns, away from the traditional industrial areas within the Central Belt and the development of large housing estates to replace previous slums. Of all the industrial changes, it is the exploitation of oil and gas in the North Sea that has had the greatest impact, especially on the coast, either in the form of extensions to existing ports, such as Aberdeen, Lerwick and

Stornoway, or new developments in quite remote locations, such as the massive oil terminals at Sullom Voe in Shetland, Flotta in Orkney and the fabrication yard at Kishorn on Loch Carron. All this has led to considerable social and cultural change, apart from the obvious economic and physical ones, in areas which have been relatively isolated from the mainstream of industrial development.

These and other shifts in the economy and in the social activities of the population have transformed communications, notably north of the Central Belt - new motorways and dual carriageways mean that Inverness is now within a few hours drive from Edinburgh - with road bridges over the Tay and the Forth Rivers. Elsewhere in the populated parts of the country there is now a web of motorways and first-class road albeit at the expense of the railway network, with many of the old lines now redesigned as walkways or cycle paths. Tourism and recreation opportunities have benefited from this new upgrading of communications, and personal mobility has been one of the most striking changes in recent years, with considerable impact on both town and countryside.

These significant movements in leisure, communications, industry, housing, forestry and agriculture have stimulated an increasing awareness of the uniqueness of the Scottish environment and the special quality of our landscapes, wildlife and historic monuments. The result has been to prompt both official and voluntary organisations to provide protection for the most important of our natural heritage resources in the form of National Nature Reserves, Sites of Special Scientific Interest, National Scenic Areas and Environmentally Sensitive Areas, and to ensure that the remaining buildings and sites of highest historic and cultural value are conserved. Much of this heritage is now acknowledged to be of international significance, and increasingly European legislation is being invoked to strengthen domestic provisions, and to emphasise Scotland's responsibilities for conservation in a global context. Indeed, the sheer extent of high quality landscape and wildlife, notably in the Highlands, poses a real problem in the selection of areas for special protection.

CHAPTER 15

So Many Inhabited Solitudes...

In recent years I have been involved in introducing visitors, many from overseas, to Scotland - its landscapes, wildlife, history, culture and traditions. It is frequently the comments of these visitors which forcibly remind one of its very special attributes: familiarity tends to breed, if not contempt, then a readiness to take too much for granted. What do they say ?

"How green!"

"Look at those gardens!" (not those around mansions, but in front of modest bungalows)

"Where are all the road-side hoardings?"

"What tidy farms!"

They comment on the lack of development along our loch shores, the prettiness of the small burghs, the open views from relatively low altitudes, the quality of the light, the varied but muted colours of the landscape, the sense of security and lack of personal threat (even in the larger cities), our sense of our history and its visibility, the openness of the people. Many of the comments relating to the land and the environment reflect on our long standing national and local planning systems, which albeit negative, have at least prevented the worst of the urban sprawl which has disfigured so many settlements in North America and elsewhere.

These are the obvious good impressions - visitors are usually too polite to refer to dirt, litter, lack of well-maintained roadside picnic sites, inadequate toilet facilities, careless service, gross traffic congestion and pollution in our cities. It is not surprising that they are usually unaware of the more subtle problems such as land degradation in the hills due to overgrazing, the problems created by winter sports developments in fragile mountain environments, the feudal land laws which inhibit appropriate development, the lack of an effective system of protection for our finest scenery. They are astonished to hear about our game laws relating to ownership, but are equally surprised by the legislative controls exercised over private owners for wildlife conservation, and they marvel at the accessibility of great tracts of fine walking countryside on our doorsteps, despite our lack of National Parks. They are intrigued by the unique crofting way of life and often appreciate the coolness of our weather, envying the plenitude of fresh water which it brings. They find difficulty in understanding our systems of forestry, dominated by plantations of introduced species.

Scotland has produced two of the most outstanding internationally recognised pioneers in the field of conservation in the persons of Sir Patrick Geddes and John Muir, whose main passions were with urban and wilderness environments respectively. These concerns are still highly relevant to the situation in Scotland today, where the appropriate balance needs to be struck between these complementary aspects of our whole environment. Patrick Geddes was as much concerned with the context of ordinary people's social and working lives as with the preservation of buildings per se. A casual observer today might be forgiven, from the preoccupations of the media, for thinking that we are much more concerned about the state of the countryside, rather than the towns, more dedicated to "green" rather than "brown" issues, despite our demography; by far the greatest proportion of the population lives in urban and industrial environments.

It is difficult not to believe that at least in part this derives from the advocacy of the more affluent, whose social and economic circumstances allow them the relative luxury of supporting green rural issues, from opposition to ski developments to supporting the system of Sites of Special Scientific Interest. The success of voluntary organisations such as the John Muir Trust testify to our 20th century middle-class love affair with the wilderness, while the Royal Society for the Protection of Birds claims a membership greater than the Conservative and Labour parties combined. A major challenge is to reconcile the antipathy which exists in some quarters between town and country, based on outmoded stereotypes and fuelled on the one hand by the perceived threat of urban values and lifestyles overwhelming rural dwellers, and on the other, of a countryside peopled by a superior "green wellie" brigade anxious to preserve their feudal privileges at the expense of the industrial proletariat.

The conundrum to be solved is how to equate even short-term local employment opportunities with longer term, national environmental objectives. This comes into particularly sharp focus where developments are proposed within areas of the highest landscape and wildlife interest, and which immediately galvanises the more articulate, often relatively well-heeled incoming retirees, into well-organised action. Without in any way relegating the causes espoused (from seal culling to the erection of fences to protect pinewoods), these must often be seen as remote as the moon in their relevance to the day-to-day lives of many people coping with damp housing, vandalised schools, and dependency on a threadbare public transport system, not to mention long-term unemployment. With the widening gap between the affluent and the poorest sections of society (by no means confined to the cities) there is a similar gap between the minority who have the resources to enjoy the best of Scotland's environment, whether urban or countryside, and the many who are effectively disempowered from influencing their own domestic, physical, economic and social circumstances. As one of the "raiding party" of young lads from inner Edinburgh who came into my garden complained:

"We dinnae hae gairdens whaur we come frae"

They might have been good candidates for the new Environmental Youth Work Development Project Scotland, the main aim of which is to use environmental involvement for the personal and social development of young people. The last phrase is particularly relevant to Scotland and the circumstances described above, since one of the early lessons learned in the initiation of this project was the necessity to avoid a prescribed environmental agenda in the first instance, and to start with the needs and aspirations of young people themselves. It goes without saying that there is within this the key element of environmental education which Scotland has pioneered in some important ways, for example, in recognising at an early stage the links between development education and sustainable development - that buzzword of the mid-Nineties. Scotland was also unusual in that the initial support for environmental education arose from urban planning rather than from a rural perspective. This is of course entirely consistent with the environmental educational concerns of Patrick Geddes who articulated the direct connections between environmental standards and quality of life, more especially for city dwellers.

Just as in other fields of education, it is now being acknowledged that improvements in techniques and standards of teaching by themselves may be much less important than raising material living standards throughout the community. Certainly there is a great deal of evidence in Scotland that concern for the environment, beyond the immediately domestic one, is related to the quality of the latter (as is diet, health, and longevity) and the associated general level of education. There is little point in exhorting the unemployed, trapped in a sub-standard inner city home to support campaigns for sustainable forestry or the protection of the Green Belt from industrial encroachment. The plain fact of the matter is that in Scotland, as elsewhere, the means of subsistence will always be a first priority where this is under threat, and so-called environmentalists have too often been guilty of adopting an indifference to this. For its part, both Central and Local Government has frequently paid lip-service to the desirability of environmental education, while refusing to commit sufficient resources or indeed to frame integrated policies to ensure that such education is given an appropriate priority.

What affluent and poor alike share to a large extent are those environmental impacts from which there is little or no escape, such as pervasive air pollution or traffic congestion. Of all the environmental issues in Scotland, whether urban or rural, this is probably the one which most overtly affects the largest number of people in their daily lives, but paradoxically, may be the most intractable. Partly this is due to the relatively low proportion of the population who are currently private car owners, but with one of the highest rates of new car acquisition in Europe, this proportion is likely to grow rapidly, especially in an expanding economy. The effects of this are already obvious in cities such as Edinburgh where pollution levels from vehicle exhausts at busy intersections frequently exceed prescribed European limits. With the present reluctance of car owners to forego the freedom of their private transport, coupled with the present inconvenience of the public alternative, this will be the litmus test of our willingness to match expressed environmental concern with individual action.

At the other end of the environmental spectrum, it is ironic that Scotland, the birthplace of John Muir, and the acknowledged founder of the American National Parks system – and by extension, National Parks throughout the world – should be one of the very few countries which does not itself have such a system of internationally recognised protected areas for its finest landscapes: it had to wait until September 1997 for the first intimation of a proposed National Park covering Loch Lomond and the Trossachs, but which will not become a reality until after the establishment of a Scottish Parliament some time after the year 2,000. There are many historic and current reasons given why this should be so, including the opposition not only of landowners, but also of some conservationists (even the John Muir Trust itself) who have expressed concern about increasing public pressure on such designated areas and land nationalisation. What is certainly true is that in the absence of such recognition, a number of areas such as the Cairngorms and Loch Lomondside and the Trossachs, to name but two, suffer from fragmented policies and lack of coherent long-term management, quite apart from inadequate funding. The two examples quoted include two quite different townships - Balloch and Aviemore - which are monuments to low quality planning and development, albeit from different eras, but which are symptomatic of a lack of appreciation of their superb surroundings, conveying a poor image as gateways to their respective areas.

What is not so frequently recognised is that apart from the protection of their physical environments, such national identification gives expression to a whole range of attributes associated with these areas - their history, their culture, the activities of the inhabitants, even their peculiar place in our mythology and folk memory, language and song. They are places in which we might take a legitimate pride (listen to any American singing the praises of Yellowstone or the Giant Redwoods) as part of our national patrimony and therefore sense of nationhood. Further, as the then Chairman of the International Union for the Conservation of Nature, Harold Eidsvik, said some 10 years ago, specifically in relation to Canada:

"There is a need to shift our political attitudes into recognising that wilderness ....is a priceless inheritance which has a legitimate place within a national strategy of sustaining social and economic well being."

That statement could equally be applied to Scotland, accepting that we may no longer have 'wilderness' as such, but we do have a need for strictly protected areas, which in the words of another commentator: ".....provide a social value as the best places to learn restraint."

There is no reason why Scotland could not develop a comprehensive system of National Parks, including marine areas, which while meeting international criteria for selection and management, is distinctively tailored to Scottish circumstances and requirements.

The effective protection of such areas inevitably raises the issue of private ownership which has been referred to in an earlier chapter. It must be acknowledged that some of our finest natural areas, including a number of National Nature Reserves, have been secured through the stewardship of private owners over considerable periods of time, often from a concern to pass on this inheritance intact to their successors. However, as a result of taxation and economic pressures, that security has been progressively eroded, traditional estates have been broken up, and the rapid re-sale of important natural areas (often to companies or interests from outside Scotland) has raised concerns about their future. Increasingly, land is regarded simply as a saleable commodity with no guarantee, under the present laissez faire system, of continuity of stewardship or long term conservation. More often than not, the owner is absent from his property, other than for a few weeks in the year when he is engaged in sport - a situation which would not be tolerated in most other countries in Western Europe and which has been a major cause for complaint in rural communities. There is no obligation on an owner, no matter how large landholding, to manage his land for the public good, unless it is within a statutory conservation area, where the requirements will be limited to wildlife considerations, and not, for example, for any community benefit.

One approach which could obviate the disadvantages of irresponsible ownership and the limitations of state ownership, would be to develop the present system of negotiated agreements under much stricter conditions. Subject to appropriate incentives and the condition that the landowner spends an appropriate period of time in residence each year, these agreements could run permanently with the land irrespective of changes in ownership. The present situation would be greatly improved by a compulsory land register and a more general regulation of land management under a broad code of practice.

The problems of private ownership and current economics come into sharp focus in the last great semi-wilderness in this country - the uplands. Overgrazing and associated burning of the hills over very long periods of time have degraded vegetation and soils, not ameliorated by the present Common Agricultural Policy system of subsidies based on the number of stock. At the same time, the number of sheep farms is falling, with many fewer of the younger generation prepared to follow this way of life, and with important consequences for this ecosystem. The problems of increasing populations of red deer, in the absence of any natural predators, have also become a matter for serious concern. Combined with the limited control over large-scale industrial forestry, these issues have raised questions about the long-term health of some of our remaining wild lands, and about the need for both land reform and regulation of management with less dependency on the so-called "voluntary principle" which has been only very partially successful. It is difficult to avoid the conclusion that a far more radical approach is now required to safeguard the public interest over a very large proportion of Scotland's mountain and moorland country.

Ultimately, the justification for such action must be the quality of the natural heritage of Scotland. We need to remind ourselves of the sheer diversity of its landscapes and wildlife over an astonishingly small area, reflecting the variety of rocks and climatic variation from east to west, and from sea level to mountain top, not to mention the distinctive island ecologies. 'Unique' is an overused word, but it can justifiably be applied to such special ecosystems as the western coastal machair, the blanket bogs of Caithness and Sutherland, the most oceanic native Scots pinewoods in the world, and the dwarf shrub heaths of our moorlands. This biodiversity, which emerged as a key theme from the UN Earth Summit at Rio de Janeiro in 1992, has for many years been an important principle underpinning the selection and management of designated natural areas in Scotland.

More recent research has shown how the patterns of distribution of flora and fauna can be used to identify coherent biogeographic zones from their indicator species. These zones in turn have helped to delineate natural heritage zones which can provide a strategic framework linking the specific protection of areas of highest natural interest to the conservation of the countryside at large. Often such zones correspond to land quality and the economic and social circumstances of their local populations, providing an opportunity to link sustainable conservation policies to the needs of the communities involved, connecting **land** and **people**.

In 1803 Dorothy Wordsworth underlined the word *inhabited*

when she referred to Scotland's 'solitudes' but less than a century later she would surely have replaced this with *uninhabited*, especially in the Highland area where she spent most of her travel time. A more contemporary view was given by the Canadian writer Hugh MacLennan when he said:

".....in a deserted Highland glen you feel that everyone who ever mattered is dead and gone."

That feeling is very much part of the folk memory of Scotland, not least in the crofting areas, and for those who aspire to protect the "wilderness" (a pejorative word in some quarters) there is still an uphill battle to convince fragile communities that their interests are being seriously considered.

This may be the most crucial element in any consideration of the future for Scotland's land – developing across the *whole* community an understanding that this capital asset is a common resource, private ownership notwithstanding, which requires a national commitment for its long term security. That commitment can only be built on a genuine sense of its contribution to the culture and well-being of rural and urban communities alike, and the development of a value system going beyond today's immediate material preoccupations. Culture here is emphasised, to highlight a common misconception that the environment is primarily to do with science and technology, when in fact it is indivisible from such aspects of our social life as language, art, music, literature and perhaps, as in the Gaelic word *dualchas* referred to previously,

---

SIR PATRICK GEDDES 1854-1932

Although Patrick Geddes was originally a botanist, becoming Professor of Botany at Dundee, he made his name as a pioneer in imaginative social and town planning, with a number of publications on the development of cities in their regional contexts. He established the Outlook Tower on Castlehill (now occupied by the Camera Obscura and a Patrick Geddes Centre) in Edinburgh as an experiment in sociology, town planning and ecology, and subsequently became Professor of Civics and Sociology at Bombay University. As a pioneer in environmental education, Geddes attempted to put his ideas into practice in creating improved environmental and social conditions in run-down parts of the Old Town of Edinburgh, founded on his innovative concepts of the linkages between quality of life at work, leisure and in the home. In his holistic approach, he anticipated aspects of the modern environmental movement, not least in recognising the importance of urban green spaces and their educational and social value.

---

a sense of our personal identity, rooted in place. It was the noted Scottish post-Enlightenment sage, Thomas Carlyle who expressed it most succinctly:

"The great law of culture is: let each become all that he was created capable of being."

– which is perhaps only Dorothy Wordsworth's sentiments expressed in a different way and to which we would now add women as well as men.

The modest measure of devolution in prospect as a result of the 1997 referendum holds out the hope that a Scottish Parliament, with its opportunity to frame legislation appropriate to Scotland, will turn its mind to the key issues of land reform and stewardship based on a land ethic and the principles of sustainability. Scotland has some outstanding advantages in the diversity of its natural systems, its stable and modest population set against its resources and land area, and its mature scientific, social, and cultural institutions. It is therefore unusually well-placed, perhaps uniquely, to provide international leadership in the framing of models of sustainable development and conservation. The original Scottish Enlighten -ment of the 18th and 19th centuries was characterised by a holistic view of the world of science, philosophy and culture to under-

---

JOHN MUIR 1838–1914

Born in Dunbar in East Lothian, the naturalist John Muir is revered in the United States as a pioneer in modern environmental thinking. Following emigration as a boy to the USA, he studied at Wisconsin University and was known as an ingenious mechanical inventor before he turned his interests to natural history and farming. Largely self-educated in the sciences, Muir wrote several books and articles which helped to focus attention on the need for active protection for some of the great American wildernesses and in 1892 Muir established the Sierra Club, one of the most influential environmental bodies in the world. Through his writing and oratory he was successful in securing the support of President Roosevelt for the very first National Park in the Yosemite Valley in 1905. Despite his fame elsewhere, it is not until relatively recently that Muir has been recognised in the country of his birth, now celebrated in the conservation trust bearing his name and in the John Muir Country Park near Dunbar.

"When I was a boy in Scotland I was fond of everything that was wild, and all my life I have been growing fonder and fonder of wild places and wild things..."
The Story of my Boyhood and Youth John Muir 1913

---

stand Man in Society: a new "Scottish Enlightenment" bringing together our best minds to focus on the proper relationship of the land and the people would be a most fitting vision for the start of the new millennium.

Appendix A: Some Places to Visit

The following is a short selection of interesting sites with public information facilities. A number of centres have combined interest – for example, many of the nature reserve centres cover the geology of the area as well as wildlife.

GEOLOGY

Inverpolly National Nature Reserve and Knockan Cliff Visitor Centre/Trail
Off A835, 19km/12miles NNE of Ullapool

Muir of Dinnet National Nature Reserve Visitor Centre/ Burn o' Vat Trail
On A97, between Aboyne and Ballater

Isle of Arran Heritage Museum Rosaburn, near Brodick

Fossil Grove, Victoria Park, Victoria Park Drive North, Glasgow

WOODLAND

Beinn Eighe National Nature Reserve – Anancaun Visitor Centre and Mountain Trail
W of A896/A832 junction at Kinlochewe

Harestanes Visitor Centre and Trail, Monteviot
At junction of A68 and B6400 5km/3miles N of Jedburgh

Glen Tanar National Nature Reserve and Braeloine Visitor Centre/Trails
Off B976, 3km/2miles W of Aboyne

Loch Lomond National Nature Reserve - Inchcailloch
Off B837, near Balmaha (boat from Balmaha)

Craigellachie National Nature Reserve and Trails
Off A9, immediately W of Aviemore

Rothiemurchus Estate Visitor Centre and Trails
1.6km/1mile from Aviemore on Coylumbridge Road

Highland Wildlife Park – Kingussie
Off A9 on B9152, 11km/7miles S of Aviemore

FARMING

North-East Scotland Agricultural Heritage Centre – Aden Country Park
On A950 between Old Deer and Mintlaw

Scottish Agricultural Museum – Ingliston
Off A8, 5km/3miles W of Edinburgh

Darnaway Farm Visitor Centre
Off A96, 5km/3miles W of Forres

Palgowan Open Farm
8km/5miles N of Bargrennan, off A714, near Newton Stewart

The Scottish Wool Centre – Aberfoyle
Near Aberfoyle town centre

Fife Folk Museum – Ceres
5km/3miles SE of Cupar on B939

Elmwood Agricultural College and Farm – Cupar, Fife

FORESTRY

Landmark Visitor Centre
Carrbridge
Off A9

Queen Elizabeth Forest Park Centre
Off A821, 1.6km/1mile N of Aberfoyle

Tummel Forest Centre
On B8019, 9.5km/6miles NW of Pitlochry

Scottish Forestry Heritage Park, Carrbridge
9.5km/6miles N of Aviemore

Argyle Forest Park – Benmore Visitor Centre
A815, 11 km/7miles NNW of Dunoon

Bonawe Iron Furnace Bonawe
Off A85,19km/12miles E of Oban

MARITIME AND FISHERIES

Scottish Fisheries Museum, Anstruther Harbour
16km/10miles SSE of St Andrews

Scottish Marine Museum, Harbourside, Irvine, Ayrshire

Aberdeen Maritime Museum, Provost Ross's House, Shiprow

Stromness Museum, Stromness, Orkney

Inverawe Smokery and Fisheries
On A85, 3km/2miles E of Taynuilt

ESTATES AND GAMESPORT

The Hirsel Homestead Museum and Grounds
On A697, immediately W of Coldstream

Galloway Deer Museum
On A714, 9.6km/6 miles W of New Galloway

Scottish Deer Centre
On A91.5km/3 miles W of Cupar, 19km/12 miles W of St Andrews

Braeloine Visitor Centre-see Glen Tanar above

Rothiemurchus Visitor Centre-see Rothiemurchus above

Glenlivet Estate and Ranger Service/Tomintoul Tourist
Information Centre, The Square, Tomintoul

CROFTING

Auchindrain Old Highland Township
On A83, 8km/5miles S of Inverary, Argyll

Highland Folk Museum
On A9 at Kingussie, 19km/12 miles SW of Aviemore

Lewis Black House – Arnol
24km/15 miles NW of Stornoway, Lewis

INDUSTRY

Bonawe Iron Furnace – see Bonawe above

New Lanark Visitor Centre
1.6km/1mile S of Lanark

Birkhill Fireclay Mine
Off A706 3 miles from Bo'ness

Almond Valley Heritage Centre
Off A705 near Livingston Village

Cardhu Distillery Visitor Centre
On B9102 at Knockando, Aberlour

Weavers House and Highland Tryst Museum
64 Burrell Street, Crieff
On A822

Scottish Museum of Woollen Textiles, Walkerburn
On A72 17km/9miles SE of Peebles

Lower City Mills, Perth
Near town centre, Perth

Scottish Mining Museum
At Prestongrange
On B1348, 13km/8miles E of Edinburgh

At Lady Victoria Colliery, Newtongrange
Preston Mill
Off A1 at East Linton, 9.5km/6miles W of Dunbar

POWER

Cruachan Pumped Storage Power Station Scheme
Off A85, 29km/18miles E of Oban

Pitlochry Power Station and Dam
Off A9 at Pitlochry

Hunterston Power Station
Off A78, 8km/5miles S of Largs

Torness Power Station
Off A1, 9.5km/5miles E of Dunbar

Dounreay Exhibition Centre, Dounreay
10 miles W of Thurso, signposted off A836

Appendix B: Further Reading

The Scottish Environment: Statistics
(Government Statistical Service, 1996)

The Geology of Scotland Craig, G.Y. (ed)
(Scottish Academic Press, 1990)

The Climate of Scotland: Some Facts and Figures
(HMSO, 1989)

Wildlife of Scotland Fred Halliday (ed)
(Macmillan/Scottish Wildlife Trust, 1979)

The Natural Heritage of Scotland: An Overview
(Scottish Natural Heritage, 1997)

Scotland: A Concise History James Halliday
(Gordon Wright Publishing, 1990)

Scottish Voices 1745-1960 T C Smout and Sydney Wood
(Fontana Press, 1991)

The Dictionary of Place Names in Scotland Mike Darton
(Eric Dobby Publishing, 1994)

Anatomy of Scotland: How Scotland Works Magnus
Linklater and Robin Denniston (eds)
(Chambers, 1992)

Scotland's Rural Land Use Agencies Donald Mackay
(Scottish Cultural Press, 1995)

Scotland: A Concise Cultural History Paul H Scott
(Mainstream Publishing, 1993)

The Nature of Scotland: Landscape, Wildlife and People
Magnus Magnusson and Graham White
(Canongate/Scottish Post Office Board, 1997)

Touring Guide to Scotland
(Scottish Tourist Board, 1993, new edition to be published
1998)

Some other books published by **LUATH** PRESS

NATURAL SCOTLAND

Wild Scotland

James McCarthy
ISBN 0 946487 37 5 PBK £7.50

Scotland is now recognised internationally for it's amazingly varied scenery and unique wildlife. This book provides a fascinating overview of the country's plants, animals, bird and marine life against the background of their typical natural settings.

Where are you most likely to see otters in Scotland?

When is the best time to see Scotland's orchids?

Are wild cats really wild?

Where are some of the oldest rocks in the world to be found?

In which city can you see fossil trees over 300 million years old?

Where can you be guaranteed to see, at close quarters, a peregrine feeding its chicks?

Where would you go to see a wild pink primrose?

Which 'animal engineer' is being considered for re-introduction to Scotland?

Wild Scotland, the site by site guide to the best of natural Scotland, answers these and many other questions.

This book is an indispensable and user-friendly travelling companion to anyone interested in exploring Scotland's remarkable natural heritage.

This study will help us to develop strategies to improve existing provisions and capitalise on potential development in an environmentally sensitive way

TOM BUNCLE, Chief Executive, Scottish Tourist Board, commenting on the recent report which described 'wildlife tourism' as one of the biggest growth sectors in the tourist industry, generating £60m in revenues annually, and supporting over 10,000 jobs.

...a visitor's guide with a very distinct difference. Jim McCarthy makes a knowledgeable, unobtrusive and surefooted guide and mentor across the length and breadth of Scotland and its islands.

MAGNUS MAGNUSSON, KBE, Chairman, Scottish Natural Heritage, from his foreword to *Wild Scotland*.

Rum: Nature's Island

Magnus Magnusson KBE
ISBN 0 946487 32 4 £7.95 PBK

Rum: Nature's Island is the fascinating story of a Hebridean island from the earliest times through to the Clearances and its period as the sporting playground of a Lancashire industrial magnate, and on to its rebirth as a National Nature Reserve, a model for the active ecological management of Scotland's wild places.

Thoroughly researched and written in a lively accessible style, the book includes comprehensive coverage of the island's geology, animals and plants, and people, with a special chapter on the Edwardian extravaganza of Kinloch Castle. There is practical information for visitors to what was once known as 'the Forbidden

Isle'; the book provides details of bothy and other accommodation, walks and nature trails. It closes with a positive vision for the island's future: biologically diverse, economically dynamic and ecologically sustainable.

LUATH GUIDES TO SCOTLAND

'Gentlemen, We have just returned from a six week stay in Scotland. I am convinced that Tom Atkinson is the best guidebook author I have ever read, about any place, any time.'
Edward Taylor, LOS ANGELES

These guides are not your traditional where-to-stay and what-to-eat books. They are companions in the rucksack or car seat, providing the discerning traveller with a blend of fiery opinion and moving description. Here you will find *'that curious pastiche of myths and legend and history that the Scots use to describe their heritage... what battle happened in which glen between which clans; where the Picts sacrificed bulls as recently as the 17th century... A lively counterpoint to the more standard, detached guidebook... Intriguing.'*
THE WASHINGTON POST

These are perfect guides for the discerning visitor or resident to keep close by for reading again and again, written by authors who invite you to share their intimate knowledge and love of the areas covered.

South West Scotland

Tom Atkinson
ISBN 0 946487 04 9 PBK £4.95
This descriptive guide to the magical country of Robert Burns covers Kyle, Carrick, Galloway, Dumfries-shire, Kirkcudbrightshire and Wigtownshire. Hills, unknown moors and unspoiled beaches grace a land steeped in history and legend and portrayed with affection and deep delight.
An essential book for the visitor who yearns to feel at home in this land of peace and grandeur.

The Lonely Lands

Tom Atkinson
ISBN 0 946487 10 3 PBK £4.95
A guide to Inveraray, Glencoe, Loch Awe, Loch Lomond, Cowal, the Kyles of Bute and all of central Argyll written with insight, sympathy and loving detail. Once Atkinson has taken you there, these lands can never feel lonely. 'I have sought to make the complex simple, the beautiful accessible and the strange familiar,' he writes, and indeed he brings to the land a knowledge and affection only accessible to someone with intimate knowledge of the area.
A must for travellers and natives who want to delve beneath the surface.
'Highly personal and somewhat quirky... steeped in the lore of Scotland.'
THE WASHINGTON POST

The Empty Lands

Tom Atkinson
ISBN 0 946487 13 8 PBK £4.95
The Highlands of Scotland from Ullapool to Bettyhill and Bonar Bridge to John O'Groats are landscapes of myth and legend, 'empty of people, but of nothing else that brings delight to any tired soul,' writes Atkinson. This highly personal guide describes Highland history and landscape with love, compassion and above all sheer magic. Essential reading for anyone who has dreamed of the Highlands.

Roads to the Isles

Tom Atkinson
ISBN 0 946487 01 4 PBK £4.95
Ardnamurchan, Morvern, Morar, Moidart and the west coast to Ullapool are included in this guide to the Far West and Far North of Scotland. An unspoiled land of mountains, lochs and silver sands is brought to the walker's toe-tips (and to the reader's fingertips) in this stark, serene and evocative account of town, country and legend.
For any visitor to this Highland wonderland, Queen Victoria's favourite place on earth.

Highways and Byways in Mull and Iona

Peter Macnab

ISBN 0 946487 16 2 PBK £4.25

'The Isle of Mull is of Isles the fairest,
Of ocean's gems 'tis the first and rarest.'

So a local poet described it a hundred years ago, and this recently revised guide to Mull and sacred Iona, the most accessible islands of the Inner Hebrides, takes the reader on a delightful tour of these rare ocean gems, travelling with a native whose unparalleled knowledge and deep feeling for the area unlock the byways of the islands in all their natural beauty.

WALK WITH LUATH

The highly respected and continually updated guides to the Cairngorms.

'Particularly good on local wildlife and how to see it.'

THE COUNTRYMAN

Walks in the Cairngorms

Ernest Cross

ISBN 0 946487 09 X PBK £3.95

This selection of walks celebrates the rare birds, animals, plants and geological wonders of a region often believed difficult to penetrate on foot.

Ideal for walkers of all ages and skiers waiting for snowier skies.

Short Walks in the Cairngorms

Ernest Cross

ISBN 0 946487 23 5 PBK £3.95

Cross wrote this volume after overhearing a walker remark that there were no short walks for lazy ramblers in the Cairngorm region. Here is the answer: rambles through scenic woods with a welcoming pub at the end, birdwatching hints, glacier holes, or for the fit and ambitious, scrambles up hills to admire vistas of glorious scenery. Wildlife in the Cairngorms is unequalled elsewhere in Britain, and here it is brought to the binoculars of any walker who treads quietly and with respect.

Mountain Days & Bothy Nights

Dave Brown and Ian Mitchell

ISBN 0 946487 15 4 PBK £7.50

Acknowledged as a classic of mountain writing still in demand ten years after its first publication, this book takes you into the bothies, howffs and dosses on the Scottish hills. Fishgut Mac, Desperate Dan and Stumpy the Big Yin stalk hill and public house, evading gamekeepers and Royalty with a camaraderie which was the trademark of Scots hillwalking in the early days.

'The fun element comes through... how innocent the social polemic seems in our nastier world of today... the book for the rucksack this year.'

Hamish Brown, SCOTTISH MOUNTAINEERING CLUB JOURNAL

The Joy of Hillwalking

Ralph Storer

ISBN 0 946487 28 6 PBK £7.50

'Alps, America, Scandinavia, you name it – Storer's been there, so why the hell shouldn't he bring all these various and varied places into his observations... [He] even admits to losing his virginity after a day on the Aggy Ridge... Well worth its place alongside Storer's earlier works.'

TAC

MUSIC AND DANCE

Highland Balls and Village Halls

GW Lockhart

ISBN 0 946487 12 X PBK £6.95

Acknowledged as a classic in Scottish dancing circles throughout the world. Anecdotes, Scottish history, dress and dance steps are all included in this book.

'A delightful survey of Scottish dancing and custom. Informative, concise and opinionated, it guides the reader across the history and geography of country dance.'

Fiddles & Folk

GW Lockhart

ISBN 0 946487 38 3 PBK £7.95

From Dougie MacLean, Hamish Henderson, the Battlefield Band, the Whistlebinkies, the Scottish Fiddle Orchestra, the McCalmans and many more come the stories that break down the musical barriers between Scotland's past and present, and between the diverse musical forms which have woven together to create the dynamism of the music today.

BIOGRAPHY

On the Trail of Robert Service

GW Lockhart

ISBN 0 946487 24 3 PBK £7.95

Known worldwide for his verses 'The Shooting of Dan McGrew' and 'The Cremation of Sam McGee', Service has woven his spell for Boy Scouts and learned professors alike. He chronicled the story of the Klondike Gold Rush, wandered the United States and Canada, Tahiti and Russia to become the bigger-than-life Bard of the Yukon. Whether you love or hate him, you can't ignore this cult figure. The book is a must for those who haven't yet met Robert Service.

Bare Feet and Tackety Boots

Archie Cameron

ISBN 0 946487 17 0 PBK £7.95

The island of Rum before the First World War was the playground of its rich absentee landowner. A survivor of life a century gone tells his story. Factors and schoolmasters, midges and poaching, deer, ducks and MacBrayne's steamers: here social history and personal anecdote create a record of a way of life gone not long ago but already almost forgotten. This is the story the gentry couldn't tell.

The authentic breath of the pawky, country-wise estate employee.'
THE OBSERVER

Come Dungeons Dark

John Taylor Caldwell

ISBN 0 946487 19 7 PBK £6.95

The welcome and long-awaited biography of... one of this country's most prolific radical propagandists... Crank or visionary?... whatever the verdict, the Glasgow anarchist has finally been given a fitting memorial.'
THE SCOTSMAN

POETRY

Blind Harry's Wallace

William Hamilton of Gilbertfield

ISBN 0 946487 43 X HBK £15.00
ISBN 0 946487 33 2 PBK £7.50

The original story of the real braveheart, Sir William Wallace. Racy, blood on every page, violently anglophobic, grossly embellished, vulgar and disgusting, clumsy and stilted, a literary failure, a great epic.

Whatever the verdict on BLIND HARRY, this is the book which has done more than any other to frame the notion of Scotland's national identity. Despite its numerous 'historical inaccuracies', it remains the principal source for what we now know about the life of Wallace.

The novel and film *Braveheart* were based on the 1722 Hamilton edition of this epic poem.

Poems to be Read Aloud

selected and introduced by Tom Atkinson

ISBN 0 946487 00 6 PBK £5.00

This personal collection of doggerel and verse ranging from the tear-jerking 'Green Eye of the Yellow God' to the rarely-printed bawdy 'Eskimo Nell' has a lively cult following. Much borrowed and rarely returned, this is a book for reading aloud in very good company, preferably after a dram or twa. You are guaranteed a warm welcome if you arrive at a gathering with this little volume in your pocket.

FOLKLORE

The Supernatural Highlands

Francis Thompson

ISBN 0 946487 31 6 PBK £8.99

An authoritative exploration of the otherworld of the Highlander, happenings and beings hitherto thought to be outwith the ordinary forces of nature. A simple introduction to the way of life of rural Highland and Island communities, this new edition weaves a path through second sight, the evil eye, witchcraft, ghosts, fairies and other supernatural beings, offering new sight-lines on areas of belief once dismissed as folklore and superstition.

HISTORY
The Bannockburn Years
William Scott
ISBN 0 946487 34 0 PBK £7.95

Written with pace and passion, William Scott has devised an original vehicle for looking at the future of Scotland. He presents, for the first time, a convincing explanation of how the victory at Bannockburn was achieved, with a rigorous examination of the history as part of the story.

Winner of the 1997 Constable Trophy, the premier award in Scotland for an unpublished novel, this book offers new insigts to both the general and academic reader, sure to provoke further discussion and debate.

'... a brilliant storyteller ... I shall expect to see your name writ large hereafter.'
NIGEL TRANTER, October 1997

SOCIAL HISTORY
The Crofting Years
Francis Thompson
ISBN 0 946487 06 5 PBK £6.95

This book fills a blank in the written history of crofting over the last two centuries. Bloody conflicts and gunboat diplomacy, treachery, compassion, music and story: all figure in this mine of information on crofting in the Highlands and Islands of Scotland.

'I would recommend this book to all who are interested in the past, but even more so to those who are interested in the future survival of our way of life and culture.'
STORNOWAY GAZETTE

Luath Press Limited
committed to publishing well written books worth reading

LUATH PRESS takes its name from Robert Burns, whose little collie Luath (*Gael.*, swift or nimble) tripped up Jean Armour at a wedding and gave him the chance to speak to the woman who was to be his wife and the abiding love of his life. Burns called one of *The Twa Dogs* Luath after Cuchullin's hunting dog in Ossian's Fingal. Luath Press grew up in the heart of Burns country, and now resides a few steps up the road from Burns' first lodgings in Edinburgh's Royal Mile.
Luath offers you distinctive writing with a hint of unexpected pleasures.

Most UK bookshops either carry our books in stock or can order them for you. To order direct from us, please send a £sterling cheque, postal order, international money order or your credit card details (number, address of cardholder and expiry date) to us at the address below. Please add post and packing as follows: UK – £1.00 per delivery address; overseas surface mail – £2.50 per delivery address; overseas airmail – £3.50 for the first book to each delivery address, plus £1.00 for each additional book by airmail to the same address. If your order is a gift, we will happily enclose your card or message at no extra charge.

Luath Press Limited
543/2 Castlehill
The Royal Mile
Edinburgh EH1 2ND
Telephone: 0131 225 4326
Fax: 0131 225 4324
email: gavin.macdougall@luath.co.uk
Website: www.luath.co.uk